Table of Contents

P9-ECV-381

Welcome to Interactions/Mosaic Silver Edition

Interactions/Mosaic **Silver Edition** is a fully-integrated, 18-book academic skills series. Language proficiencies are articulated from the beginning through advanced levels <u>within</u> each of the four language skill strands. Chapter themes articulate <u>across</u> the four skill strands to systematically recycle content, vocabulary, and grammar.

NEW to the Silver Edition:

- **World's most popular and comprehensive academic skills series**—thoroughly updated for today's global learners
- **Full-color design** showcases compelling instructional photos to strengthen the educational experience
- **Enhanced focus on vocabulary building, test taking, and critical thinking skills** promotes academic achievement
- **New Self-Assessment Logs** encourage students to evaluate their learning
- **New "Best Practices" approach** in Teacher's Edition promotes excellence in language teaching

SILVER EDITION

Interactions ACCESS

READING

Pamela Hartmann
James Mentel

Lawrence J. Zwier
Contributor, Focus on Testing

Pamela Hartmann
Reading Strand Leader

Interactions Access Reading, Silver Edition

Published by McGraw-Hill ESL/ELT, a business unit of The McGraw-Hill Companies, Inc. 1221 Avenue of the Americas, New York, NY 10020. Copyright © 2007 by The McGraw-Hill Companies, Inc. All rights reserved. No part of this publication may be reproduced or distributed in any form or by any means, or stored in a database or retrieval system, without the prior written consent of The McGraw-Hill companies, Inc., including, but not limited to, in any network or other electronic storage or transmission, or broadcast for distance learning.

ISBN 13: 978-0-07-340634-3 (Student Book)
ISBN 10: 0-07-340634-1
1 2 3 4 5 6 7 8 9 10 VNH 11 10 09 08 07 06

Editorial director: Erik Gundersen
Series editor: Valerie Kelemen
Developmental editor: Terre Passero
Production manager: Juanita Thompson
Production coordinator: Vanessa Nuttry
Cover designer: Robin Locke Monda
Interior designer: Nesbitt Graphics, Inc.
Artists: Burgundy Beam
Photo researcher: Photoquick Research

The credits section for this book begins on page iv and is considered an extension of the copyright page.

Cover photo: Mark Andrew Kirby/Lonely Planet Images
A peacock mosaic from the Udaipur City Palace and Museum in the Rajasthan region of India.

www.esl-elt.mcgraw-hill.com

The McGraw·Hill Companies

A Special Thank You

The Interactions/Mosaic Silver Edition team wishes to thank our extended team: teachers, students, administrators, and teacher trainers, all of whom contributed invaluably to the making of this edition.

Macarena Aguilar, **North Harris College**, Houston, Texas ■ Mohamad Al-Alam, **Imam Mohammad University**, Riyadh, Saudi Arabia ■ Faisal M. Al Mohanna Abaalkhail, **King Saud University**, Riyadh, Saudi Arabia; Amal Al-Toaimy, **Women's College, Prince Sultan University**, Riyadh, Saudi Arabia ■ Douglas Arroliga, **Ave Maria University**, Managua, Nicaragua ■ Fairlie Atkinson, **Sungkyunkwan University**, Seoul, Korea ■ Jose R. Bahamonde, **Miami-Dade Community College**, Miami, Florida ■ John Ball, **Universidad de las Americas**, Mexico City, Mexico ■ Steven Bell, **Universidad la Salle**, Mexico City, Mexico ■ Damian Benstead, **Sungkyunkwan University**, Seoul, Korea ■ Paul Cameron, **National Chengchi University**, Taipei, Taiwan R.O.C. ■ Sun Chang, **Soongsil University**, Seoul, Korea ■ Grace Chao, **Soochow University**, Taipei, Taiwan R.O.C. ■ Chien Ping Chen, **Hua Fan University**, Taipei, Taiwan R.O.C. ■ Selma Chen, **Chihlee Institute of Technology**, Taipei, Taiwan R.O.C. ■ Sylvia Chiu, **Soochow University**, Taipei, Taiwan R.O.C. ■ Mary Colonna, **Columbia University**, New York, New York ■ Lee Culver, **Miami-Dade Community College,** Miami, Florida ■ Joy Durighello, **City College of San Francisco**, San Francisco, California ■ Isabel Del Valle, **ULATINA**, San Jose, Costa Rica ■ Linda Emerson, **Sogang University**, Seoul, Korea ■ Esther Entin, **Miami-Dade Community College**, Miami, Florida ■ Glenn Farrier, **Gakushuin Women's College**, Tokyo, Japan ■ Su Wei Feng, Taipei, Taiwan R.O.C. ■ Judith Garcia, **Miami-Dade Community College**, Miami, Florida ■ Maxine Gillway, **United Arab Emirates University**, Al Ain, United Arab Emirates ■ Colin Gullberg, **Soochow University**, Taipei, Taiwan R.O.C. ■ Natasha Haugnes, **Academy of Art University**, San Francisco, California ■ Barbara Hockman, **City College of San Francisco**, San Francisco, California ■ Jinyoung Hong, **Sogang University**, Seoul, Korea ■ Sherry Hsieh, **Christ's College**, Taipei, Taiwan R.O.C. ■ Yu-shen Hsu, **Soochow University**, Taipei, Taiwan R.O.C. ■ Cheung Kai-Chong, **Shih-Shin University**, Taipei, Taiwan R.O.C. ■ Leslie Kanberg, **City College of San Francisco**, San Francisco, California ■ Gregory Keech, **City College of San Francisco**, San Francisco, California ■ Susan Kelly, **Sogang University**, Seoul, Korea ■ Myoungsuk Kim, **Soongsil University**, Seoul, Korea ■ Youngsuk Kim, **Soongsil University**, Seoul, Korea ■ Roy Langdon, **Sungkyunkwan University**, Seoul, Korea ■ Rocio Lara, **University of Costa Rica**, San Jose, Costa Rica ■ Insung Lee, **Soongsil University**, Seoul, Korea ■ Andy Leung, **National Tsing Hua University**, Taipei, Taiwan R.O.C. ■ Elisa Li Chan, **University of Costa Rica**, San Jose, Costa Rica ■ Elizabeth Lorenzo, **Universidad Internacional de las Americas**, San Jose, Costa Rica ■ Cheryl Magnant, **Sungkyunkwan University**, Seoul, Korea ■ Narciso Maldonado Iuit, **Escuela Tecnica Electricista**, Mexico City, Mexico ■ Shaun Manning, **Hankuk University of Foreign Studies**, Seoul, Korea ■ Yoshiko Matsubayashi, **Tokyo International University**, Saitama, Japan ■ Scott Miles, **Sogang University**, Seoul, Korea ■ William Mooney, **Chinese Culture University**, Taipei, Taiwan R.O.C. ■ Jeff Moore, **Sungkyunkwan University**, Seoul, Korea ■ Mavelin de Moreno, **Lehnsen Roosevelt School**, Guatemala City, Guatemala ■ Ahmed Motala, **University of Sharjah**, Sharjah, United Arab Emirates ■ Carlos Navarro, **University of Costa Rica**, San Jose, Costa Rica ■ Dan Neal, **Chih Chien University**, Taipei, Taiwan R.O.C. ■ Margarita Novo, **University of Costa Rica**, San Jose, Costa Rica ■ Karen O'Neill, **San Jose State University**, San Jose, California ■ Linda O'Roke, **City College of San Francisco**, San Francisco, California ■ Martha Padilla, **Colegio de Bachilleres de Sinaloa,** Culiacan, Mexico ■ Allen Quesada, **University of Costa Rica**, San Jose, Costa Rica ■ Jim Rogge, **Broward Community College**, Ft. Lauderdale, Florida ■ Marge Ryder, **City College of San Francisco**, San Francisco, California ■ Gerardo Salas, **University of Costa Rica**, San Jose, Costa Rica ■ Shigeo Sato, **Tamagawa University**, Tokyo, Japan ■ Lynn Schneider, **City College of San Francisco**, San Francisco, California ■ Devan Scoble, **Sungkyunkwan University**, Seoul, Korea ■ Maryjane Scott, **Soongsil University**, Seoul, Korea ■ Ghaida Shaban, **Makassed Philanthropic School**, Beirut, Lebanon ■ Maha Shalok, **Makassed Philanthropic School**, Beirut, Lebanon ■ John Shannon, **University of Sharjah**, Sharjah, United Arab Emirates ■ Elsa Sheng, **National Technology College of Taipei**, Taipei, Taiwan R.O.C. ■ Ye-Wei Sheng, **National Taipei College of Business**, Taipei, Taiwan R.O.C. ■ Emilia Sobaja, **University of Costa Rica**, San Jose, Costa Rica ■ You-Souk Yoon, **Sungkyunkwan University**, Seoul, Korea ■ Shanda Stromfield, **San Jose State University**, San Jose, California ■ Richard Swingle, **Kansai Gaidai College**, Osaka, Japan ■ Carol Sung, **Christ's College**, Taipei, Taiwan R.O.C. ■ Jeng-Yih Tim Hsu, **National Kaohsiung First University of Science and Technology**, Kaohsiung, Taiwan R.O.C. ■ Shinichiro Torikai, **Rikkyo University**, Tokyo, Japan ■ Sungsoon Wang, **Sogang University**, Seoul, Korea ■ Kathleen Wolf, **City College of San Francisco**, San Francisco, California ■ Sean Wray, **Waseda University International**, Tokyo, Japan ■ Belinda Yanda, **Academy of Art University**, San Francisco, California ■ Su Huei Yang, **National Taipei College of Business**, Taipei, Taiwan R.O.C. ■ Tzu Yun Yu, **Chungyu Institute of Technology**, Taipei, Taiwan R.O.C.

Author Acknowledgements

This edition is dedicated to Beatrice Hartmann,
an inspiration and buoy.

Photo Credits

Page v (t to b): Jose Fuste Raga/CORBIS, H. Sitton/CORBIS, Franco Vogt/CORBIS, Royalty-Free/CORBIS, Corinne Malet/PhotoAlto, Philippe Psaila/Photo Researchers, Reuters/CORBIS, Digital Vision/PunchStock, H. Sitton/CORBIS, Frans Lanting/ CORBIS; viii: H. Sitton/CORBIS; ix (tl): Jules Frazier/Getty Images; ix (tr): Royalty-Free/CORBIS; ix (b): PhotoLink/Getty Images; x (t): The Fat Kitchen by Steen, Jan Havicksz. (1625/26-79) © Cheltenham Art Gallery & Museums, Gloucestershire, UK/The Bridgeman Art Library; x (b): JupiterImages; xi: Andersen Ross/Getty Images; xii (t to b): Jose Fuste Raga/CORBIS, H. Sitton/CORBIS, Franco Vogt/CORBIS, Tony Freeman/Photoedit; xiv (t to b): Corinne Malet/PhotoAlto, Philippe Psaila/Photo Researchers, Reuters/CORBIS, Digital Vision/PunchStock; xvi (t to b): H. Sitton/ CORBIS, Frans Lanting/ CORBIS; 3: Jose Fuste Raga/CORBIS; 10: Tony Freeman/ PhotoEdit; 11: The McGraw-Hill Companies/Luke David;15: Getty Images; 21: H. Sitton/CORBIS; 25 (t): Amazon.com; 25 (b): Tannen Maury/The Image Works; 28 (l): TRBfoto/Getty Images; 28 (r): Brand X Pictures/PunchStock; 29 (both); Royalty-Free/ CORBIS; 39: Franco Vogt/CORBIS; 40: Corbis/PunchStock; 42: Novastock/ PhotoEdit; 43 (t): Tina Manley/Alamy; 43 (b): White Rock/Getty Images; 44: Andersen Ross/Getty Images; 47 (t): PhotoLink/Getty Images; 47 (bl): Digital Vision/Getty Images; 47 (br): Don Tremain/Getty Images; 50: Ken Usami/Getty Images; 57: Royalty-Free/CORBIS; 58 (t to b): Ryan McVay/Getty Images, Getty Images, Royalty-Free /CORBIS, Karl Weatherly/Getty Images, Nancy R. Cohen/Getty Images, Getty Images/Digital Vision, The McGraw-Hill Companies/Joe DeGrandis, Nick Koudis/Getty Images; 60 (tl): PhotoLink/Getty Images: 60 (tr): Ross Anania/Getty Images; 60 (b): PhotoLink/Getty Images; 65: Getty Images/Digital Vision; 71 (t to b) : Dynamic Graphics/JupiterImages, Laurent/Dielundama/Photo Researchers, image100/age fotostock, PhotoLink/Getty Images, Getty Images, Corbis/JupiterImages; 77: Corinne Malet/PhotoAlto; 95: Philippe Psaila/Photo Researchers; 96: Corbis/PictureQuest; 99: Royalty-Free/CORBIS; 104: Ryan McVay/Getty Images; 113: Lucas Jackson/Reuters/CORBIS; 114 (tl): Photo by Tim McCabe, USDA Natural Resources Conservation Service; 114 (tr): image100/ PunchStock; 114 (b): Brand X Pictures/PunchStock; 116:: Jim Sugar/CORBIS; 117: Reuters/CORBIS; 120 (l): Karen Huntt/CORBIS; 120 (r): Charles O'Rear/CORBIS; 131: Digital Vision/PunchStock; 134 (t): The Fat Kitchen by Steen, Jan Havicksz. (1625/26-79) © Cheltenham Art Gallery & Museums, Gloucestershire, UK/The Bridgeman Art Library; 134 (b): JupiterImages; 138 (l to r); Creatas/PunchStock, Royalty-Free/CORBIS, image100/PunchStock; 139: Product of Hotlix ® 2006 www.hotlix.com-Graphic design & photography www.yrigollen.com; 144: Creatas/PunchStock; 149: H. Sitton/CORBIS; 150 (tl): PhotoLink/Getty Images; 150 (tr): Royalty-Free/CORBIS; 150 (bl): Digital Vision; 150 (br): Ryan McVay/Getty Images; 153: James L. Amos/CORBIS; 154 (t): Creatas/PunchStock; 154 (b): David R. Frazier/Photo Researchers; 155: Wolfgang Kaehler/CORBIS; 158 (l): Royalty-Free/CORBIS; 158 (tr): Digital Vision; 158 (br): Hisham F. Ibrahim/Getty Images; 162 (t): Steve Mason/Getty Images; 162 (b): Robert Holmes/CORBIS; 163 (t): Pixtal/Superstock; 163 (b): eStock Photo/Jupiterimages; 169: Frans Lanting/CORBIS; 170 (tl): Jules Frazier/Getty Images; 170 (tr): Royalty-Free/ CORBIS; 170 (b): PhotoLink/Getty Images; 173: Royalty-Free/CORBIS; 178: Brand X Pictures/PunchStock; 179 (tl): Josh Westrich/CORBIS; 179 (tr): C Squared Studios/ Getty Images; 179 (b): Photodisc/Getty Images.

Interactions/Mosaic
Best Practices

Our Interactions/Mosaic Silver Edition team has produced an edition that focuses on Best Practices, principles that contribute to excellent language teaching and learning. Our team of writers, editors, and teacher consultants has identified the following six interconnected Best Practices:

M aking Use of Academic Content

Materials and tasks based on academic content and experiences give learning real purpose. Students explore real world issues, discuss academic topics, and study content-based and thematic materials.

O rganizing Information

Students learn to organize thoughts and notes through a variety of graphic organizers that accommodate diverse learning and thinking styles.

S caffolding Instruction

A scaffold is a physical structure that facilitates construction of a building. Similarly, scaffolding instruction is a tool used to facilitate language learning in the form of predictable and flexible tasks. Some examples include oral or written modeling by the teacher or students, placing information in a larger framework, and reinterpretation.

A ctivating Prior Knowledge

Students can better understand new spoken or written material when they connect to the content. Activating prior knowledge allows students to tap into what they already know, building on this knowledge, and stirring a curiosity for more knowledge.

I nteracting with Others

Activities that promote human interaction in pair work, small group work, and whole class activities present opportunities for real world contact and real world use of language.

C ultivating Critical Thinking

Strategies for critical thinking are taught explicitly. Students learn tools that promote critical thinking skills crucial to success in the academic world.

Highlights of Interactions Access/ Reading Silver Edition

Full-color design showcases compelling instructional photos to strengthen the educational experience.

Interacting with Others
Questions and topical quotes stimulate interest, activate prior knowledge, and launch the topic of the unit.

Chapter

2

Shopping and e-Commerce

Connecting to the Topic

1. What are the people in the photo shopping for? What are they saying to each other?
2. What do you like to shop for?
3. Where do you usually shop?

In This Chapter

Where do you like to shop? In Part 1 of this chapter, you will read about shopping on the Internet and the future of shopping. Which website was one of the first to sell products online? Read about that and the person who started it in Part 2. If you shop online, it's important to create safe passwords. In Part 3, you will learn about creating a safe password for websites. Then in Part 4, you will have a chance to work more with new vocabulary.

❝ The safe way to double your money is to fold it over once and put it in your pocket. ❞

—Frank McKinney Hubbard
American writer, humorist (1868–1930)

Part 1	Reading Skills and Strategies

The Ocean in Trouble

Before You Read

1 Thinking About the Topic Look at the photos and answer the questions.

▲ Seafood for restaurants   ▲ Fishers repairing their nets

▲ Commercial fishing trawler with its nets

1. Describe each photo. What do you see?

2. Which countries have a lot of coastline, lakes, and rivers? Do you think fishing is important in those places?

3. Do you eat a lot of seafood? Do you think people eat more seafood now than they ate in the past? If so, why?

4. Do you know of any problems for the fishing industry?

2 Previewing Vocabulary Read the words in the list. They are words from the next reading. Listen to their pronunciation. Do not look them up in a dictionary. Check (✓) the words that you know.

Nouns	Verbs	Adjectives	Preposition
❑ amount	❑ catch	❑ extinct	❑ but
❑ areas	❑ create	❑ fake	
❑ crabs	❑ destroy		
❑ damage	❑ drag		
❑ danger	❑ influence		
❑ dolphins	❑ police		
❑ environmentalists	❑ pressure		
❑ methods	❑ prove		
❑ nets	❑ reproduce		
❑ overfishing	❑ urged		
❑ trawlers	❑ warning		
❑ whales			
❑ zones			

3 Finding the Meaning of Words from Context Find the meanings of the underlined words. Look at the sentence or phrase before or after the word for help.

1. George loves to eat, and he likes all kinds of food. He'll eat anything <u>but</u> insects because he thinks they're disgusting.
   - Ⓐ however
   - Ⓑ except for
   - Ⓒ and

2. The large boat <u>dragged</u> another small boat behind it through the water.
   - Ⓐ pulled
   - Ⓑ pushed
   - Ⓒ repaired

3. Our great-grandparents sometimes saw that species, but now we can't because it's <u>extinct</u>, like the dinosaurs.
   - Ⓐ hard to find
   - Ⓑ completely dead
   - Ⓒ only in zoos

4. After the people of the city <u>pressured</u> the government, the government built a new road.
   - Ⓐ caused worry to
   - Ⓑ caused stress to
   - Ⓒ put a lot of stress on

New Foods, New Diets

Diet of the Past

A   On March 26, 1662, Samuel Pepys and four friends had lunch at his home in London, England. They ate beef, cheese, two kinds of fish, and six chickens. Today, we might wonder, "What? No fruits? No vegetables?" More than 300 years ago, people in Europe ate differently from today. They looked different, too. In famous paintings by Titian, Rubens, and other artists, people weren't thin; they were overweight. But people 300 years ago thought, "How attractive!"—not, "How ugly!"

▲ People in a 16th century painting

Today's Diet

B   Today, people are learning more about health. Many people are changing their ways of eating. They're eating a lot of fruits and vegetables. Many of the vegetables are raw. They aren't cooked because cooking takes away some vitamins, such as vitamins A, B, and C. People are eating less sugar. They're eating low-fat foods. They're not eating much red meat. They're drinking less cola and coffee.

Trying to Be Thin

C   People these days want to be slim, not fat. Sometimes people in North America go a little crazy to lose pounds. Thousands of them join gyms and diet groups, go to special diet doctors, or spend a lot of money at diet centers. Each year Americans spend more than $46 billion on diets and diet products.

▲ People in a modern health club

More People Are Overweight

D   However, there is an irony—a surprising, opposite result—to all this dieting. While many people are becoming thin, other people are becoming overweight. More people are overweight than in the past! In many countries, there is a serious problem with obesity—in other words, a condition of being very overweight. There are two main reasons. First, these days, many people often go to fast-food restaurants. (They didn't in the past.) At these restaurants, many of the foods (such as fried potatoes and meat) are high in fat. Some of the dairy products (such as cheese) are high in fat, and others (such as ice cream) are high in fat and sugar. This seems similar to Samuel Pepys's party, doesn't it? Second, dieting doesn't often work. Sometimes people lose weight fast, but they usually gain it back again. Almost 95 percent of all people gain back weight after a diet. One problem with obesity is easy to see: overweight people have more sicknesses, such as heart disease and diabetes.

E   Sometimes people go crazy over food. Sometimes they eat very little because they want to be slim. Other times, they eat lots of bad foods because these foods taste good. When will people learn? Too much food, too little food, and the wrong foods are all bad ideas.

Culture Note

Vegetarians
Vegetarians are people who don't eat meat. Some vegetarians don't eat dairy products, either. In what countries or cultures is it easy to be a vegetarian? In what countries or cultures is it hard? If you are a vegetarian, why did you decide to be one? If you are not a vegetarian, would you consider becoming one?

After You Read

6 Identifying the Topics Read the topics below. Which paragraph is about each topic? Write the letter of the paragraph next to its topic.

1. _____ spending a lot of time and money on diets
2. _____ how people in Europe ate in the past
3. _____ conclusion
4. _____ a serious problem with weight in some countries
5. _____ foods for good health

7 Working with New Words Write the vocabulary words for the meanings below. For help, look back at the boldfaced words in the reading.

Paragraph	Meaning	Vocabulary Word
A	two famous painters	
D	a surprising, opposite result	
D	at the same time	
D	a condition of being very overweight	
D	a word for products from milk	
D	a sickness	

Organizing Information
Graphic organizers provide tools for organizing information and ideas.

alone. The number of single-parent families is going up, too. In Denmark, 60 percent of all first-born children have parents who are not married. 50

F   The world is changing, and families are changing, too. There are many new types of families, but most seem to be getting smaller. 55

▲ A single-parent family

After You Read

6 Identifying the Main Ideas Complete the sentences. Choose the best answer.

1. The main idea is that _____
   - (A) in North Africa, families are big, but in Europe, they're small
   - (B) families around the world are changing
   - (C) there is more divorce today than in the past

2. The writer thinks that new families are _____
   - (A) good because they are small
   - (B) different from families in the past
   - (C) bad because people don't live together

UNDERSTANDING PRONOUNS
Pronouns are words such as *he, she, it, they, this, that, these,* or *those.* Pronouns take the place of nouns. Look before the pronoun to find the noun that it replaces. That will help you to understand the pronoun's meaning.

Example My grandfather lived with us. **He** is there in the photo, on the right.
(*He* refers to "My grandfather.")

7 Understanding Pronouns Find the meaning of each underlined pronoun. Highlight it. Then draw an arrow from the pronoun to its meaning.

1. Fifty to a hundred people lived together in a group of houses. These were all family members.

2. One generation ago, the average Mexican woman had seven children. Today, she has an average of only 2.5 children.

3. Many men and women spend a lot of time at work. They don't spend much time together as a family.

4. They don't spend much time together as a family. This can be very difficult.

5. Many young women don't want this kind of marriage. They get a job and live with their parents.

6. Many Europeans don't get a divorce, but they don't get *married*, either.

Strategy

Understanding Organization in an Article or Essay
An essay has a main topic and a main idea. (The topic of the first reading in this chapter is *families*. The main idea is that *families are getting smaller*.) Essays also have subtopics—smaller parts of the main topic. Each subtopic has a main idea, too. Many articles and essays are organized in this way:

Paragraph A: Introduction of the topic and the main idea of the article or essay
Paragraph B: Subtopic, main idea, and details
Paragraph C: Another subtopic, main idea, and details
Paragraph D: Another subtopic, main idea, and details
Paragraph E: Another subtopic, main idea, and details
Paragraph F: Conclusion (restates the main idea of the essay)

8 Understanding Organization in an Essay: Using a Graphic Organizer Fill in this graphic organizer with the topic and the main idea from each paragraph of the reading on pages 42–44. Use your words or copy from the reading.

Paragraph	Topic	Main Idea
A	families	All over the world, families are getting smaller.
B		
C		Mexican families are getting smaller.
D		
E		
F	families	

9 Thinking Critically: Finding Reasons Discuss the following questions. Make a list of possible reasons for each. Then share your answers with the class.

1. Why are families in some countries smaller than in the past?
2. Why are there more single-parent families now?

Scaffolding Instruction
Instruction and practice with new language structures helps students increase their reading fluency.

Cultivating Critical Thinking
Enhanced focus on critical thinking skills promotes academic achievement.

Scope and Sequence

Critical Thinking Skills	Vocabulary Building	Language Skills
Synthesizing and discussing ideas from a reading Compare personal experiences	Previewing vocabulary Understanding new words with *is* or *are* Categorizing new words Working with prepositions Identifying opposites	Understanding large numbers Working with prepositions
Analyzing predictions from the past and about the future Identifying a good summary Synthesizing and discussing ideas from a reading Safely using passwords on websites	Previewing vocabulary Understanding new words from examples Understanding new words: using punctuation clues	Reviewing verb tenses
Finding reasons Making predictions Synthesizing and discussing ideas from a reading Using a graphic organizer to organize ideas in an essay	Previewing vocabulary Understanding new words: using pictures Using a dictionary: alphabetical order Understanding pronouns Using *get* and *have*	Interviewing other students Understanding pronouns
Analyzing and comparing answers Finding important details Synthesizing and discussing ideas from a reading	Previewing vocabulary Finding meaning after *which* or *who* Identifying and matching vocabulary words and definitions Understanding pronouns Changing nouns to adjectives Identifying body parts Identifying opposites	Giving advice Understanding guide words in a dictionary Describing illnesses Understanding pronouns

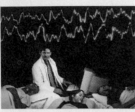

Critical Thinking Skills	Vocabulary Building	Language Skills
Understanding humor Understanding mood Making predictions Analyzing different perspectives	Previewing vocabulary Checking vocabulary	Interviewing other students Discussing ideas from the reading Understanding language and sexism Using gender-neutral possessive adjectives
Understanding mood Finding the meaning of new words from context Searching for and analyzing information on the Internet	Previewing vocabulary Understanding words from their parts Finding the meaning of words: meaning after *or* Previewing vocabulary Understanding pronouns	Interviewing students Discussing ideas from the reading Understanding pronouns
Organizing details using a T-chart Making inferences Reading and analyzing a chart	Previewing vocabulary Understanding words from their parts: suffixes	Understanding sentences with the word *that*
Organizing details using a graphic organizer Reading and analyzing a chart Analyzing information	Previewing vocabulary Using opposites to understand a new word Figuring out words with more than one meaning	Interviewing other students

Critical Thinking Skills	Vocabulary Building	Language Skills
Reaching a conclusion: paying attention to evidence	Previewing vocabulary	Understanding words for directions
Synthesizing and discussing ideas from a reading	Understanding words for directions	Stating and explaining opinions
Reading a website and analyzing information	Understanding words from their prefixes	
Identifying support for opinions	Using *go* + verb + *-ing* for activities	
Understanding relationships between ideas	Previewing vocabulary	Interviewing other students
Using a graphic organizer show relationships	Understanding words from their parts: *over* in a word	Using facts and figures
Making inferences	Understanding words that can be more than one part of speech	
Discussing and synthesizing the reading		
Reading and analyzing a graph		
Reading and analyzing a pie chart		
Comparing facts and figures		

1

Neighborhoods, Cities, and Towns

Do you live in a big or a small city? In Part 1 of this chapter, you will read about very big cities around the world. You will discuss likes and dislikes about cities. In Part 2, you will read about a student's neighborhood and discuss your own. You will practice reading a map of a large, famous city in Part 3. Last, in Part 4, you will practice Chapter 1 vocabulary, work with opposites and pronouns, and do a crossword puzzle.

❝ What is the city but the people? ❞

—William Shakespeare
English playwright (1564–1616)

1. What do you see in this photo?

2. Name ten adjectives to describe this city.

3. Do you like big or small cities? Explain why.

Monster Cities

Before You Read

1 **Thinking About the Topic** Discuss these questions with a partner.

1. Look at the picture below. What do you see?

2. Describe your home city or town. What do you like about it?

3. What do you like about cities? What do you dislike?

▲ Do you live in a monster city?

Strategy

Scanning

You can scan a reading to find information quickly. Follow these steps to scan:

- Know the information that you want to find.
- Look for that information.
- Move your eyes quickly across the words. Don't read every word.

You will practice scanning throughout the book when you look for specific information and details.

2 Previewing Vocabulary Read the words in the list. They are words from the next reading. Listen to their pronunciation. Do not look them up in a dictionary. Check (✓) the words that you know.

Nouns
- ❏ cities (city)
- ❏ countries (country)
- ❏ crime
- ❏ density
- ❏ megacity
- ❏ monster

- ❏ people
- ❏ population

Verbs
- ❏ growing
- ❏ move
- ❏ work

Adjectives
- ❏ afraid
- ❏ busy
- ❏ crowded
- ❏ different
- ❏ dirty
- ❏ large

- ❏ small
- ❏ terrible
- ❏ wonderful

Strategy

Understanding New Words: Look for *Is* and *Are*

You do not always need to use a dictionary to find the meaning of a new word. Sometimes the meaning of a new word comes after the word *is* or *are* in the sentence.

Example

Population **is** the number of people in a city or country.
(Population = the number of people in a city or country.)

---

3 Understanding New Words with *Is* The meanings of these words are in the next article. Find the words and circle their meanings.

monster	megacity	density

Read

4 Reading an Article Read the following article. Then do the exercises.

Monster Cities

A   Are big **cities wonderful** places? Are they **terrible**? There are **different** ideas about this. William H. Whyte writes books about cities. He is happy in a **crowded** city. He loves **busy** streets with many stores and many **people**. He likes the life in city parks and restaurants.

B Many people don't like big cities. They see the **large population** of cities, and they are **afraid**. Many cities are **growing** very fast. They are "**monster**" cities. (A monster is a big, terrible thing.) In some **countries**, there are no jobs in **small** towns. People go to cities to **work**. For example, 300,000 people go to São Paulo, Brazil, every year. In China, about 183,000 people **move** to Beijing from the countryside every year. São Paulo and Beijing are both **megacities**. 5 10

C A **megacity** is a very, very big city. It includes the main city and the cities and towns around it. Mexico City is a megacity. It has a population of about 8,600,000 in the city itself, but there are more than 21,000,000 people in the megacity. Tokyo is another megacity, with over 8,200,000 people in Tokyo, but over 31,000,000 in Tokyo and the cities around it. London is another megacity. There are about 7,400,000 people in London, and about 18,400,000 in London and the surrounding towns and cities. 15

D There are problems in all cities. There are big (or *mega*) problems in a megacity. In many U.S. cities, there are many people with no jobs and no homes. The air is **dirty**. There are too many cars. A terrible problem is crime. Many people are afraid of crime. People want to feel safe. 20

E Population **density** is the number of people in one square mile (2.59 square kilometers). Population density is a big problem in many cities. In Miami, Florida, the density is only 7,748. In Bangkok, Thailand, there are 58,397 people per square mile. Is this crowded? Yes! But other cities are more crowded. Do you think William H. Whyte likes Hong Kong? The population density there is 247,501! 25 30 35

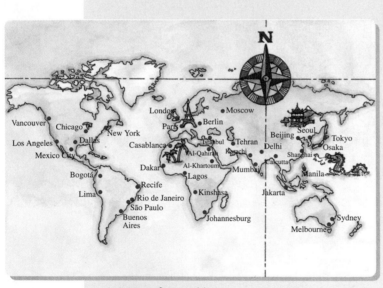

▲ Map of megacities

After You Read

5 **Identifying the Main Ideas** Complete the sentences. Choose the best answer for each blank.

1. "Monster Cities" is about _____.
- Ⓐ the large number of small cities
- Ⓑ the number of people in U.S. cities
- Ⓒ the problems of very big cities

2. Mexico City, Tokyo, and Hong Kong are three _____.

   (A) small cities

   (B) very big, crowded cities

   (C) cities with no crime or dirty air

6 **Checking Vocabulary** Write a word for each definition. Use words from the reading.

1. a big, terrible thing = _____

2. a city together with other areas around the city = _____

3. the number of people in one square mile = _____

7 **Making Good Guesses** Complete the sentence. Choose the best answer.

The word *monster* is in the title ("Monster Cities") because _____.

   (A) the writer is happy in big cities

   (B) some cities are growing too fast, and this is causing terrible problems

   (C) there are people with no jobs and no homes, and they are unhappy

8 **Discussing Ideas From the Reading** Answer these questions with a partner.

1. Is your city large or small?

2. What is the population?

3. What is nice about your city?

4. What is a problem in your city?

5. Do you like your city? Why or why not?

6. Look at the map on page 6. How many megacities are in Asia? In Africa? In Europe? In the Americas?

UNDERSTANDING LARGE NUMBERS

Look at the words for large numbers below. Read the words out loud with a partner.

150	one hundred fifty
200	two hundred
3,000	three thousand
4,500	four thousand five hundred
5,350	five thousand three hundred fifty
6,475	six thousand four hundred seventy-five
70,000	seventy thousand
80,950	eighty thousand nine hundred fifty
100,000	one hundred thousand
950,632	nine hundred fifty thousand six hundred thirty-two
1,000,000	one million
15,700,000	fifteen million seven hundred thousand
23,570,600	twenty-three million five hundred seventy thousand six hundred

9 Understanding Large Numbers: Information Gap Follow these directions:

Step 1: Work with a partner. One of you is Student A. One is Student B.
Step 2: Student A looks at this page. Student B looks at page 9.
Step 3: Follow the directions on your page.

Student A

Step 1: Ask your partner the questions below.
Step 2: Write your partner's answers in the chart.

Questions

1. What is the population of Shanghai (the megacity)?

2. What is the population of Mumbai (the city)?

3. What is the population of Seoul (the megacity)?

4. What is the population of Dubai (the city)?

5. What is the population of Mexico City (the megacity)?

6. What is the population of New York (the city)?

7. What is the population of London (the megacity)?

Populations of Large Cities		
City, Country	The City (2004)	The Megacity
Shanghai, China	9,005,600	
Mumbai (Bombay), India		17,012,900
Buenos Aires, Argentina	12,116,400	13,076,300
Seoul, Korea	9,630,600	
Dubai, United Arab Emirates		1,511,700
Jakarta, Indonesia	8,827,900	17,891,000
Mexico City, Mexico	8,681,400	
Tokyo, Japan	8,240,100	31,139,900
New York, U.S.A.		21,766,731
London, U.K.	7,417,700	

Student B

Step 1: Ask your partner the questions below.

Step 2: Write your partner's answers in the chart.

Questions

1. What is the population of Shanghai (the city)?
2. What is the population of Buenos Aires (the megacity)?
3. What is the population of Dubai (the megacity)?
4. What is the population of Jakarta (the city)?
5. What is the population of Mexico City (the city)?
6. What is the population of Tokyo (the city)?
7. What is the population of New York (the megacity)?

Populations of Large Cities		
City, Country	The City (2004)	The Megacity
Shanghai, China		12,039,900
Mumbai (Bombay), India	12,383,100	17,012,900
Buenos Aires, Argentina	12,116,400	
Seoul, Korea	9,630,600	19,969,100
Dubai, United Arab Emirates	906,100	
Jakarta, Indonesia		17,891,000
Mexico City, Mexico		21,233,900
Tokyo, Japan		31,139,900
New York, U.S.A.	8,085,742	
London, U.K.	7,417,700	11,219,000

Part 2   Reading Skills and Strategies

My Neighborhood in the United States

Before You Read

1 Thinking About the Topic Look at the photo on page 10. What kind of neighborhood is this? Busy? Interesting? Crowded? What country do you think it is in?

▲ Does this look like your neighborhood?

2 **Previewing Vocabulary** Read the words in the list. They are words from the next reading. Listen to their pronunciation. Do not look them up in a dictionary. Check (✓) the words that you know.

Nouns	**Verb**	**Prepositions**
❏ address	❏ live	❏ across
❏ building		❏ from
❏ corner		❏ in
❏ neighborhood		❏ in front of
❏ neighbors		❏ on
❏ oak tree		
❏ olive tree		

Read

3 **Reading an Essay** Read the following essay. Then do the exercises.

My Neighborhood

A   My name is Elena Sanchez. I'm **from** Mexico, but now I **live in** California. I'm a student here in English language classes at a small college.

B   I live in an apartment **building**. It's **on** the **corner** of Olive Street and Sycamore Avenue. My **address** is 2201 Olive Street. There's a big **olive tree in front of** the building. There's a park **across** the street. There are a 5 lot of **oak trees** in the park. The trees are beautiful in the summer.

▲ A neighborhood store in California

C   A lot of my **neighbors** are from different countries. The people next to me are from Indonesia. The family across from the Indonesian family is from Colombia.   10

D   The stores in this **neighborhood** are always busy. There's a Korean drugstore and an Armenian flower shop. A Chinese church is next to the flower shop. There are three restaurants on Olive Street: one   15 Mexican, one Japanese, and one Moroccan–Italian–American!

E   I like my neighborhood, but I ask myself one question. Where are the Americans?   20

Culture Note

Neighborhoods in Large Cities
Many large cities in North America have neighborhoods with many people from other countries. Two examples are Chinatown in New York City and Koreatown in Los Angeles. Do large cities in your home country have different neighborhoods? What kinds of people live in those neighborhoods?

After You Read

4 Identifying the Main Idea What is the main idea of the essay? Choose one answer.

  (A) Elena studies English in a college in California.
  (B) The people in Elena's neighborhood are from many countries.
  (C) There are restaurants with food from many countries in Elena's neighborhood.

5 Understanding Details Read Elena's story again. Then look at the map of her neighborhood. Answer the question on page 12.

▲ Elena's neighborhood

Where are these places? Write the letters from the map on the lines.

1. the Indonesian family's house __D__

2. the Japanese restaurant _____

3. the Chinese church _____

4. the park _____

5. the Colombian family's house _____

DIRECTIONS IN TEXTBOOKS

Read the following directions and look at the examples. You will find directions like these in your textbook exercises.

Directions	Example
1. Circle the word.	(building)
2. Copy the word.	street *street*
3. Underline the word.	building
4. Circle the letter of the answer.	Which word is a country? a. Texas (b.) Mexico c. park
5. Fill in the blank.	My name __is__ Elena.
6. Write your name on the line.	___Elena Vasquez___
7. Correct the mistakes.	She's from mexio.
8. Choose the best answer.	Which place is a city? (A) Seoul (B) Indonesia (C) Japan

6 **Following Textbook Directions** Now follow these textbook directions.

1. Circle the name of a city.
   Brazil   Indonesia   Tokyo   Egypt

2. Find the name of a person below and copy it.

   Mexico _____   California _____

   the USA _____   Elena _____

3. Underline the word for a building.
   I'm at a restaurant now.

4. Circle the letter of a kind of restaurant in Elena's neighborhood.
   a. Chinese   b. Mexican   c. Korean   d. Indonesian

5. Write the name of your country on the line. _____

6. Correct the mistakes.
   I live in colomba.

7. Choose the name of a country.

   (A) Armenian
   (B) Italian
   (C) Japan
   (D) Moroccan

7 **Building Vocabulary** Write the words from the box in the correct places on the chart.

American	flower shop	Korean
apartment building	Indonesia	Mexican
Armenian	Indonesian	Moroccan
church	Italian	oak
Colombia	Japan	olive
drugstore	Japanese	restaurant

Countries	Indonesia,
Trees	oak,
Words that mean *from a country* or *of a country*	Italian,
Buildings	restaurant.

8 **Completing Sentences** Fill in each blank with a word from the box.

building	different	neighbors
crowded	front	neighborhood

1. This store is always _____. There are always lots and lots of people.

2. There is a big apartment _____ on the corner.

3. There are two schools in my _____.

4. My _____ are from Mexico. They're nice people.

5. There are two big trees in _____ of my house.

6. People in my neighborhood are from _____ countries.

9 **Discussing the Reading** Discuss these questions with a group.

1. What stores are in your neighborhood?

2. Are there people from different countries in your neighborhood? What countries are they from?

3. Draw a map of your neighborhood. Describe it to your group.

10 **Writing in Your Journal** Choose one topic below. Write about it for five minutes. Use some of the vocabulary that you have learned in this chapter.

- your neighborhood (Describe it.)
- big cities (Do you like them? Why or why not?)
- your favorite city (Describe it.)
- some problems in your city (Describe them.)
- why the population is so big in one city (Choose one city.)

Part 3 Practical English

Maps

1 **Reading a Map** Look at the map below. Answer these questions.

1. What is the name of this big city? _____

2. What country is this city in? _____

3. What do you call people who live in this country? _____

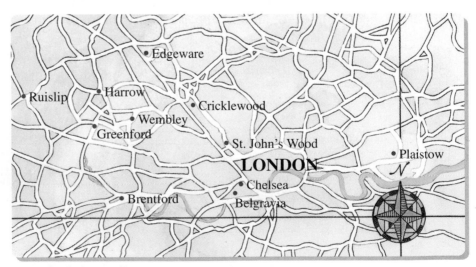

▲ London is a megacity.

4. Find the town of Wembly on the map. Then complete these sentences.

a. Wembly is _____*west*_____ of Cricklewood.

b. Wembly is _____ of Greenford.

c. Wembly is _____ of Edgeware.

d. Wembly is _____ of Ruislip.

5. Now read this description of a city on the map. What city is it?

This city is north of Belgravia, east of Chelsea, and southeast of St. Johns Wood. This city is called _____.

2 **Reading a Map: A Closer Look** Look at the map of a part of London below. Read the descriptions below the map. Write the place in the blank.

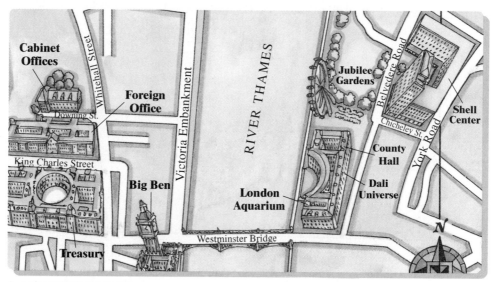

▲ A closer look at London

1. It's at the end of Victoria Embankment south of the Westminster Bridge. It's on the west side of the Thames River. *Big Ben* _____

2. It's on King Charles Street, across from the Treasury. It's west of the Department of Health & DWP building. _____

3. It's on Downing Street, north of the Foreign Office. _____

4. It's part of County Hall, next to Dalí Universe, on the east side of the Thames River, just north of Westminster Bridge. _____

5. It's across from the Shell Center, on the Thames River, on Belvedere Road. It's just north of County Hall. _____

1 Working with Prepositions This chapter uses a lot of prepositions. Fill in the blanks with one of the four prepositions in the box below.

across	from	in	on

1. I live ___in___ Mexico.

2. I am _____ Hong Kong, but I live in Singapore.

3. The park is _____ the street from the market.

4. He is _____ Guatemala but he lives _____ the United States now.

5. Maria lives _____ Olive Street, _____ a big apartment building.

6. Tokyo is _____ Japan.

7. Many people _____ El Salvador live _____ my street, here in Los Angeles.

8. Many Armenians live _____ this neighborhood.

9. This is the most crowded neighborhood _____ New York.

10. Jung lives _____ a house _____ the street _____ from my apartment building.

2 Identifying Opposites Read the words in Column A. Write the opposite of each word in the blank in Column B. Use the words from the box.

afraid	dirty	love	small
busy	grow	monster	terrible

Column A

1. large

2. wonderful

3. empty or quiet

4. relaxed, not scared

5. average person or thing

6. clean

7. hate

8. get smaller

Column B

1. _____ small

2. _____

3. _____

4. _____

5. _____

6. _____

7. _____

8. _____

3 Listening: Focusing on Prepositions Listen and fill in the words from the reading on page 10. Then check your work. All of the missing words are prepositions.

My name is Elena Sanchez. I'm _____ Mexico, but now I live
                                              1
_____ California. I'm a student here in English language classes
      2
_____ a small college.
      3

I live _____ an apartment building. It's _____ the corner
                  4   5
of Olive Street and Sycamore Avenue. My address is 2201 Olive Street. There's
a big olive tree _____ front _____ the building. There's a park
                        6   7
_____ the street. There are a lot of oak trees _____ the
      8   9
park. The trees are beautiful _____ the summer.
                                      10

4 Focusing on High-Frequency Words Read the paragraph below and fill in each blank with a word from the box. When you finish, check your answers on page 6.

population	people	growing	cities	move	work

Many people don't like big _____. They see the large
                                      1
_____ of cities, and they are afraid. Many cities
      2
are _____ very fast. They are "monster" cities.
            3
(A monster is a big, terrible thing.) In some countries, there are no
jobs in small towns. People go to cities to _____. For
                                                         4
example, 300,000 _____ go to São Paulo, Brazil, every
                          5
year. In China, about 183,000 people _____ to Beijing
                                                    6
from the countryside every year. São Paulo and Beijing are both megacities.

5 Building Vocabulary Complete the crossword puzzle with words from the box. Read the clues and write the words in the puzzle. These words are from Chapter 1.

address	Japanese	terrible
copy	monster	wonderful
crowded	people	
density	population	

Across

4. write the same thing (v.)

5. very, very good (adj.)

8. having lots of people in one place (adj.)

9. the number of people in one square mile (n.)

10. men, women, and children (n.)

Down

1. from Japan (adj.)

2. where you live; for example, 1432 Main Street (n.)

3. the number of people who live in a city (n.)

6. very, very bad (adj.)

7. "Look! There's a _____. I'm afraid." (n.)

KEY: *adj.* = adjective; *adv.* = adverb; *n.* = noun; *prep.* = preposition; *v.* = verb

Self-Assessment Log

Read the lists below. Check (✓) the strategies and vocabulary that you know. Look through the chapter or ask your instructor about the other strategies and words.

Reading and Vocabulary-Building Strategies

❏ Scanning
❏ Previewing vocabulary
❏ Understanding new words: look for *is* and *are*
❏ Identifying the main ideas
❏ Understanding large numbers
❏ Understanding details
❏ Following textbook directions
❏ Reading a map
❏ Working with prepositions
❏ Identifying opposites

Target Vocabulary

Nouns

❏ address*
❏ building*
❏ cities (city)*
❏ countries (country)*
❏ density
❏ megacity
❏ monster
❏ neighbors*
❏ neighborhood

❏ oak trees
❏ olive tree
❏ people*
❏ population*
❏ tree*
❏ work*

Verbs

❏ growing*
❏ live*
❏ move*
❏ work*

Adjectives

❏ afraid
❏ busy
❏ crowded*
❏ different*
❏ dirty
❏ large*
❏ small*
❏ terrible
❏ wonderful*

Prepositions

❏ across
❏ from
❏ in
❏ in front of
❏ on

*These words are among the 1,000 most-frequently used words in English.

Shopping and e-Commerce

In This Chapter

Where do you like to shop? In Part 1 of this chapter, you will read about shopping on the Internet and the future of shopping. Which website was one of the first to sell products online? Read about that and the person who started it in Part 2. If you shop online, it's important to create safe passwords. In Part 3, you will learn about creating a safe password for websites. Then in Part 4, you will have a chance to work more with new vocabulary.

> **"** The safe way to double your money is to fold it over once and put it in your pocket. **"**
>
> —Frank McKinney Hubbard
> American writer, humorist (1868–1930)

Connecting to the Topic

1 What are the people in the photo shopping for? What are they saying to each other?

2 What do you like to shop for?

3 Where do you usually shop?

Internet Shopping

Before You Read

1 **Thinking About the Topic** Ask different classmates the questions below. Write their answers in this chart. For students who answer *yes* to a question, ask them the second question in the box.

Question	Yes	No
1. Do you have a computer? How often do you use it?		
2. Do you use the Internet? What do you use it for?		
3. Did you know about the Internet ten years ago? When did you start using the Internet?		
4. Do you shop on the Internet? What do you buy on the Internet?		

REVIEWING VERB TENSES

Regular verbs (such as *shop, start*, or *use*) end in *-ed* in the past tense, but many common verbs (such as *know*) are irregular in the past tense.

Tense	Time	Subject	Verb Phrase
Past	Five years ago,	I you he/she/it we you they	**used** the Internet.
Present	Today,	I you	**use** the Internet.
		he/she/it	**uses** the Internet.
		we you they	**use** the Internet.

Tense	Time	Subject	Verb Phrase
Future	Soon,	I you	**am going to use** the Internet. **will** use the Internet.
		he/she/it	**is going to use** it. **will use** it.
		we you	**are going to use** it. **will use** it.

2 **Reviewing the Irregular Past Tense** Read the verbs in the chart below. Fill in the past tense of each verb. (Check a dictionary for verbs that you don't know.) With a partner, write one sentence with each past tense verb.

Verb	Irregular Past Tense
be	*was, were*
begin	
buy	
drive	
have	
know	
quit	
sell	
think	

3 **Reviewing the Future Tense** Now write one future sentence with each verb from the chart above. Use *be going to*.

FYI Note

In natural spoken English, the pronunciation of *going to* is usually *gonna*.

4 **Previewing Vocabulary** Read the words in the list. They are words from the next reading. Listen to their pronunciation. Do not look them up in a dictionary. Check (✓) the words that you know.

Nouns
- ❑ categories (category)
- ❑ customers
- ❑ garage
- ❑ home improvement products
- ❑ information
- ❑ mall
- ❑ money
- ❑ prediction
- ❑ products
- ❑ profit
- ❑ scientists
- ❑ site
- ❑ stores
- ❑ percent
- ❑ virtual shopping mall

Verbs
- ❑ drove (drive)
- ❑ predict
- ❑ quit
- ❑ search
- ❑ sell

Adjectives
- ❑ gourmet
- ❑ huge
- ❑ online

Understanding New Words: Using Punctuation Clues

You do not always need to use a dictionary to find the meaning of a new word in a reading. Sometimes you can find the meaning of a new word in parentheses ( ) or after a dash —.

Examples

They sell products in many **categories** (groups of similar things).

(*categories* = groups of similar things)

People can **search for**—look for—a book on the Internet.

(*search for* = look for)

5 **Understanding New Words: Using Punctuation Clues** The meanings of these words are in the next article. Find the words and circle their meanings.

online

customers

home improvement products

virtual shopping mall

gourmet

Read

6 **Reading an Article** Read the following article. Don't use your dictionary. If you don't know some words, try to figure out their meaning. Then do the exercises.

Internet Shopping

A   Twenty-five years ago, very few people used the Internet. Only **scientists** and people in the government knew about the Internet and how to use it. This is changing very fast. Now almost everyone knows about the Internet, and many people are **online** (on the Internet) every day. When people think about the Internet, they often think about **information**. But now, more and more, when people think about the Internet, they think about shopping.   5

B   Amazon.com was one of the first companies to try to **sell products** on the Internet. Jeff Bezos started the company. One day he made a **prediction** about the future. He saw that the World Wide Web was growing 2,000   10

▲ Amazon.com web page

percent a year. He predicted that it was going to continue to grow, and he thought that shopping was going to move to the Internet. People were going to shop online. He **quit** his good job and **drove** across the country to Seattle, Washington. There he started an online bookstore called Amazon.com. Bezos had very little **money**. The company began in a **garage** (a building for a car), and at first there were very few **customers** (people who buy things). 15 20

C   At the Amazon.com **site**, people can **search** for a book about a subject, find many different books about that subject, read what other people think about the books, 25 order them by credit card, and get them in the mail in two days. This kind of bookstore was a new idea, but the business grew. In a few years, 30 Amazon.com had 10 million customers and sold 18 million different items in **categories** including books, CDs, toys, electronics, videos, DVDs, **home improvement products** (things that you use to fix up a house), software,

▲ Jeff Bezos giving a speech

and video games. Today, at a **"virtual shopping mall"** —a group of online **stores**—you can buy anything from 35 **gourmet** food—special, usually expensive food— to vacations.

D   Fifteen years ago, many people said, "Online shopping is crazy. Nobody can make money in an online company." They were wrong. Today, Jeff Bezos is a 40 billionaire. More and more people are shopping online, and online companies are making a **profit**. It is a **huge** business. But some people **predict**, "Online business isn't going to grow any more." They say, "customers are afraid of online crime, and they will stop shopping on 45 the Internet." Are these people right? Nobody knows, but we'll soon find out.

After You Read

7 Identifying the Main Ideas Complete the sentences. Choose the best answer.

1. The title of the article is "Internet Shopping." Another possible title is _____.
   - (A) "Internet Games"
   - (B) "Shopping on the Internet"
   - (C) "Information and the Internet"

2. The main idea of Paragraph A is _____.
   - (A) now more and more people use the Internet
   - (B) twenty-five years ago, very few people used the Internet
   - (C) scientists were first to use the Internet

3. The main idea of Paragraph B is _____.
   - (A) the Web was growing 2,000 percent a year
   - (B) Amazon.com is an example of a company that sells on the Internet
   - (C) Jeff Bezos quit his good job and moved to Seattle, Washington

4. The main idea of Paragraph C is _____.
   - (A) people can order books by credit card
   - (B) Amazon.com grew
   - (C) people can search for a book on Amazon.com

5. Paragraph D is about _____.
   - (A) online shopping today and in the future
   - (B) Jeff Bezos
   - (C) people's fears about online shopping

8 Building Vocabulary Write a word for each definition. Use words from the reading.

1. on the Internet = _____

2. people who buy things = _____

3. things that you use to fix up a house = _____

4. a group of online stores = _____

5. special, usually expensive food = _____ food

9 Making Good Guesses Read the sentences. Choose the best answer.

1. We bought the house for $100,000. We sold it for $110,000. We made a $10,000 profit.
   A profit is probably _____.
   - (A) money that you lose in business
   - (B) money that you make in business
   - (C) money that you pay for a house

2. Jeff Bezos had very little money. The company began in a garage, and at first there were very few customers.

A garage is probably a _____.

(A) big, expensive house

(B) place to play baseball

(C) small, inexpensive building

UNDERSTANDING QUOTATION MARKS

Use quotation marks (" ") to tell exactly what someone says.

Example Jonathon said, "Our online business is growing every year."

10 Understanding Quotation Marks Look in Paragraph D. What do some people predict? What do they say? Look for sentences in quotation marks. Copy the quotes here.

_____

_____

_____

_____

11 Discussing the Reading Discuss the following questions. Then share your answers with the class.

1. Do you or your friends spend a lot of time online? Is this good or bad?

2. Do you think Internet shopping is going to get bigger and more important in every country? Will some people stop going to stores?

Part 2 | Reading Skills and Strategies

Predicting the Future of Shopping

Before You Read

1 Thinking Ahead Look at the photos on page 28. Answer these questions.

1. What do you think the online shopper is buying?
2. What do you think the three women bought at the mall?
3. In your opinion, which photo shows the future of shopping? Why?

▲ Shopping online, from home

▲ Shopping at a mall

 2 Previewing Vocabulary Read the words in the list. They are words from the next reading. Listen to their pronunciation. Do not look them up in a dictionary. Check () the words that you know.

Nouns	Verbs	Adjectives	Adverb
❑ bags	❑ carry	❑ easy	❑ alone
❑ computers	❑ choose	❑ second	
❑ entertainment	❑ put		
❑ eye scan	❑ socialize		
❑ gym			
❑ purchases			

3 Understanding New Words from Examples The meaning of these words is in the next article. Find the words and circle their meanings.

socialize	purchases	entertainment

Read

4 **Reading an Article** Read the following article. Then do the exercises.

Predicting the Future of Shopping

A   There are different ideas about shopping in the future. Some people say, "Everybody is going to shop online, from home. There won't be any more real stores or shopping malls." But other people have a different picture of the future. They say, "There will still be shopping malls. In the future, many people will work at home, **alone**, on their **computers**. They'll 5 want to go out to stores for their shopping. They'll want to **socialize**—be with other people." Maybe they're right.

B   But the stores of the future will probably be different from stores 10 today. Shopping in stores will be **easy**. First, people won't need to **carry** many **bags** from store to store. In stores, they will only choose products. They won't carry them 15 home. The stores will deliver most of their **purchases**, such as clothes and books, to their houses. **Second**, people won't need to carry money or credit cards with them. An **eye scan** 20 will identify their eyes and **put** their purchase on their credit card.

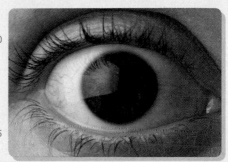

▲ In an eye scan, a computer identifies you from your eyes.

C   Shopping malls will probably also be different from today. They won't only have big department stores and 25 many small stores. Malls will still be places for shopping and for **entertainment** such as movies. But in malls of the future, busy people will also do other things. They will go to the 30

▲ People at the gym in a mall

doctor, the dentist, and the post office. They will go to the **gym**, too. Everybody agrees about one thing: shopping will be different in the future.

After You Read

Identifying the Topic and Main Idea of a Paragraph

A paragraph is about one main *topic* (subject). The topic is a *noun* or a *noun phrase* (one or more words about a person, place, or thing). A paragraph has one *main idea*—a sentence about the topic. The main idea is often the first sentence. For example, the *Internet* might be the topic of a paragraph, and the main idea might be: *The Internet is a great way to shop.*

5 **Identifying the Topic and Main Idea** Read the topics below. Write the letter of the paragraph (A, B, or C) next to each topic. Next, find the main idea of each paragraph. <u>Underline</u> the main idea in each paragraph in the reading.

_____ shopping in stores

_____ malls in the future

_____ ideas about shopping in the future

Strategy

Summarizing

A *summary* has the main information of a paragraph or an article. It also has important details, but it doesn't have small details. Look at these two summaries of "Internet Shopping" in Part 1. Answer these questions: *Which summary is good? Why?*

A. Twenty-five years ago, most people didn't know about the Internet. Only scientists and the government used it. Today almost everyone finds information and shops online. Jeff Bezos began Amazon.com in a garage. The business grew fast. Soon it had 10 million customers and sold 18 million different items. At this online store, people can buy books, CDs, toys, electronics, gourmet food, and almost anything.

B. Many people are now shopping on the Internet. One example is the online store Amazon.com. Jeff Bezos began this site with books, but now it sells many different products. Amazon.com has a lot of customers, and it is making money.

Answer: The second summary is good. It has the main idea and important details. It doesn't have small details. The first summary is not good. It has small details.

 6 **Identifying a Good Summary** Which is a good summary of the article "Predicting the Future of Shopping"? Why is it good? Why is the other not good?

A.   In the future, shopping will be different. It will be easy to shop in stores. People won't need to carry bags, money, or credit cards. In shopping malls, people will shop, find entertainment, and do practical things.

B.   In the future, people will work alone at home. They will want to go out and shop in stores. They will want to be with other people. Stores will be places to choose products. There will be eye scans in stores. Shopping malls are going to have stores, movies, doctors, dentists, post offices, and gyms.

7 **Thinking Critically** Predicting the future is a very difficult thing to do. Most people have a hard time doing this. Below are famous predictions from the past. What was wrong with each one? Discuss them with a group.

1. "I think there is a world market for maybe five computers."
      —A computer company executive, 1943

2. "No one is going to want a computer in their home."
      —A president of a large computer company, 1977

3. "Airplanes are interesting toys, but they have no military value."
      —A French professor of war, 1910

4. "Man will never reach the moon."
      —A scientist, 1952

5. "For most people, smoking is good for their health."
      —A doctor, quoted in a national magazine, 1963

8 **Discussing the Future** Below are some predictions about the next 50 years. Do you agree with them? On each line, write *likely* (will probably happen), *possible* (might happen), or *not likely* (probably won't happen). Then discuss your answers with a small group.

1. Every family will have a robot—a smart machine—to clean their house.

_____

2. Scientists are going to have a cure for cancer in ten years. _____

3. Everyone in the world is going to use the Internet every day. _____

4. A very bad disease is going to kill 50 percent of all human beings. _____

5. No one is going to read books or magazines. They are going to listen to them on digital equipment such as computers and DVD players. _____

6. No one in the world is going to smoke cigarettes._____

7. Religion is going to become more important for people. _____

8. Everyone in the world is going to be able to speak English. _____

9. China is going to be the richest country in the world. _____

9 **Writing in Your Journal** Choose one topic below. Write about it for five minutes. Use some of the vocabulary that you have learned in this chapter.

- online shopping
- shopping malls
- your prediction about shopping in the future

Part 3 Practical English

Passwords on Websites

Using the Internet

Safely Using Passwords on Websites
Many websites ask you to enter your username and password to use their sites. Your password is important. You should choose it carefully and protect it.

Follow these rules when you choose a password:

1. Don't use passwords with information that someone can easily find out, such as your name, address, phone number, or date of birth.

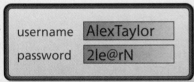
▲ A website sign-in box

2. Use passwords of at least six characters with both upper- and lower-case letters, numbers, and symbols, for example, 2le@rN.

3. Use a different password for each site you register with.

4. If you need to write down your passwords, keep them in a safe place.

5. Never tell anyone your password.

6. For important accounts, such as bank websites or websites where you use a credit card, change your passwords frequently. Some people recommend every two months.

1 **Answering Questions About Passwords** Read the questions below and choose the correct answer.

1. Which password is probably the best?
   - (A) jim07031981
   - (B) mypassword01
   - (C) &YeS$66

2. When you register with a website, you usually _____.

  (A) pay money

  (B) fill out a form

  (C) change your password

3. When you think of a password, it's a good idea to _____.

  (A) use your last name to help you remember

  (B) use both symbols (such as $ and #) and letters

  (C) use your birth date

2 **Creating a Password** Write a new password below. Do not use your birth date, address, or name for the password. At the end of the week, see if you can remember it. (Because it's now written in your book, don't use this password on a website.) Write your name or your nickname in the username box.

> username [   ]
>
> password [   ]

▲ What's an example of a safe password?

Part 4 Vocabulary Practice

1 **Answering True or False** Read these sentences. Check (✓) True or False. New words from this chapter are underlined.

	True	False
1. You put a car in a <u>garage</u>.	❏	❏
2. When you have a <u>profit</u>, you have lost money.	❏	❏
3. When you are <u>online</u>, you are using the Internet.	❏	❏
4. You can drive or walk to a <u>mall</u>.	❏	❏
5. You can drive or walk to a <u>virtual shopping mall</u>.	❏	❏
6. Some people make <u>predictions</u> about the past.	❏	❏
7. When people work at home, they often work <u>alone</u>.	❏	❏

🎧 **2 Listening: Fill in the Missing Words** Listen and fill in the words. Some of the words are new and some of the words are not new. Then check your work on page 24.

Twenty-five years _____ ₁, very few people used the _____ ₂. Only scientists and people in the government _____ ₃ about the Internet and how to use it. This is changing very fast. Now almost everyone _____ ₄ about the Internet, and many people are _____ ₅ (on the Internet) every day. When people _____ ₆ about the Internet, they often think about _____ ₇. But now, more and more, when people think _____ ₈ the Internet, they think about shopping.

3 Using New Words Write the correct word from the box in the sentences.

categories	online	profit	socialize
information	predict	scientists	summary

1. We sell products in many *categories* _____: electronics, sports equipment, and home improvement products.

2. _____ are trying to find a cure for cancer.

3. He never goes to the mall—he does all his shopping _____.

4. I go to parties and see friends a lot because I like to _____.

5. People often try to _____ the future, but they are often wrong.

6. When you study for a test, it helps to write a short _____ of what you read.

7. I use the Internet when I need _____ about something.

8. He sold the company and he made a huge _____ —twenty million dollars.

4 Focusing on High-Frequency Words Read the paragraph on the next page and fill in each blank with a word from the box. Then check your answers on page 29.

carry	easy	money	second
choose	eye	put	stores

Stores of the future will probably be different from _____ today. Shopping in stores will be
1
_____. First, people won't need to
2
_____ many bags from store to store. In stores,
3
they will only _____ products. They won't carry
4
them home. The stores will deliver most of their purchases, such
as clothes and books, to their houses. _____, people
5
won't need to carry _____ or credit cards with them.
6
An _____ scan will identify their eyes and
7
_____ their purchase on their credit card.
8

5 **Building Vocabulary** Complete the crossword puzzle with words from the box. These words are from Chapter 2. (Hint: Look for the easy answers first and fill in those words. This will help you with the more difficult words.)

bookstore	garage	percent	scientists
categories	gourmet	product	search
customers	huge	profit	site
drove	information	quit	think

Across

1. very big (adj.)
3. something you sell (n.)
5. money you can keep (n.)
6. to stop doing something (v.)
8. a place that sells books (n.)
10. groups of things (n.)
11. tell about the future (v.)
13. people who buy things (n.)
15. something you need to know (n.)
16. look for (v.)

Down

2. a place to park your car (n.)
4. something you do with your brain; (some people do this more than other people) (v.)
7. a word used to talk about food: It means "special, very good" (adj.)
9. people who work in science—biologists, physicists, geologists, medical researchers (n.)
11. a word that means this symbol: % (n.)
12. used a car (past tense) (v.)
14. a place on the Internet (n.)

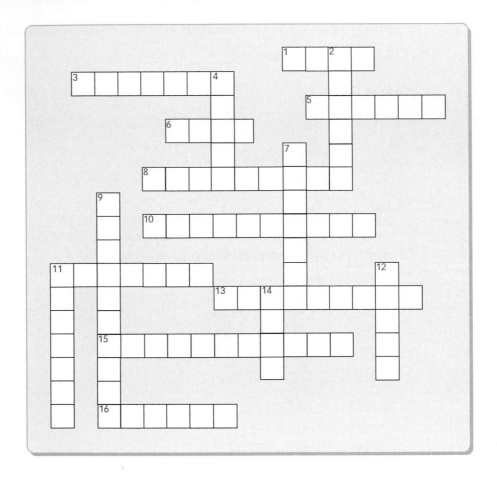

KEY: *adj.* = adjective; *adv.* = adverb; *n.* = noun; *prep.* = preposition; *v.* = verb

Self-Assessment Log

Read the lists below. Check (✓) the strategies and vocabulary that you know. Look through the chapter or ask your instructor about the other strategies and words.

Reading and Vocabulary-Building Strategies
- ❑ Reviewing verb tenses
- ❑ Previewing vocabulary
- ❑ Understanding new words: using punctuation clues
- ❑ Identifying the main ideas
- ❑ Understanding quotation marks
- ❑ Understanding new words from examples
- ❑ Identifying the topic and main idea of a paragraph
- ❑ Summarizing
- ❑ Creating passwords for websites

Target Vocabulary

Nouns
- ❑ categories (category)
- ❑ customers
- ❑ entertainment
- ❑ eye scan
- ❑ garage
- ❑ home improvement products
- ❑ information
- ❑ Internet
- ❑ mall
- ❑ money*
- ❑ prediction
- ❑ products*
- ❑ profit*
- ❑ purchases
- ❑ scientists*
- ❑ site
- ❑ stores*
- ❑ virtual shopping mall

Verbs
- ❑ choose*
- ❑ drove (drive)*
- ❑ predict
- ❑ put*
- ❑ quit
- ❑ search
- ❑ sell*
- ❑ socialize

Adjectives
- ❑ easy*
- ❑ gourmet
- ❑ huge
- ❑ online
- ❑ second*

Adverb
- ❑ alone*

* These words are among the 1,000 most-frequently used words in English.

Friends and Family

You will read how families in several countries are changing. Are families growing? Are they getting smaller? In Part 1, you will have the chance to learn about and discuss the changing size and look of families. In Part 2, you will read a young woman's story about her large family reunion. Then you will read a foreign student's blog in Part 3. Through her blog, she shares her culture and her feelings about being away from home. Part 4 provides you with the opportunity to practice new vocabulary.

❝ Call it a clan, call it a network, call it a tribe, call it a family. Whatever you call it, whoever you are, you need one. ❞

—Jane Howard
U.S. journalist, writer (1935–1996)

Connecting to the Topic

1 What are these people doing?

2 What do you think they are talking about?

3 What do you do when you are with friends and family? What do you talk about?

Changing Families

Before You Read

1 **Thinking About the Topic** Look at the photo. Then answer these questions about it. Make a guess if you aren't sure of the answers.

1. What country do you think this family is from?

2. What are their relationships to each other?

3. Do they live in a city or in the countryside?

4. What do they do for work?

▲ "Cheese!"

2 **Interviewing Other Students** Walk around the room with your book and a pencil and ask five students these questions. Write their answers in the chart below. If a student doesn't know an answer, just put a question mark (?).

Example

Maria, choose one of your grandfathers. How many brothers or sisters does he, or did he have?

How many brothers and sisters did (does) each of these people have?					
Student's Name	One of Your Grandfathers	One of Your Grandmothers	Your Father	Your Mother	You

In your chart, you have three generations (people from three age groups) in the students' families. Are families getting bigger, getting smaller, or staying the same? Share your answers.

 3 **Previewing Vocabulary** Read the words in the list. They are words from the next reading. Listen to their pronunciation. Do not look them up in a dictionary. Check (✓) the words that you know.

Nouns
- ❑ basics
- ❑ children (child)
- ❑ divorces
- ❑ generations
- ❑ extended families (family)

- ❑ marriage
- ❑ nuclear families
- ❑ single-parent families
- ❑ traditional family
- ❑ women

Adjectives
- ❑ average
- ❑ first-born
- ❑ married

Adverbs
- ❑ either
- ❑ too

Strategy

Skimming

You can skim a reading to identify the topic and main idea. When you skim, you can also try to predict or guess what the reading is about. Skimming a reading before you fully read it can help you to better understand it. Follow these steps to skim:

- Read the title and any subheadings.
- Look at photos and diagrams.
- Read the first and last line of each paragraph.
- Read quickly. Don't read every word.

You will practice skimming when you find main ideas and do previewing and predicting activities.

Understanding New Words: Using Pictures

You do not always need to use a dictionary to find the meaning of a new word. Sometimes pictures can help you to find the meaning of a new word. Look at the photo below. Read the caption. What do you think *divorce* means?

▲ Divorce is common in some countries.

4 Understanding New Words: Using Pictures Before you read the next article, look at the photos to find the meaning of these words. Write the meanings on the lines.

1. extended family: _____

2. nuclear family: _____

3. single-parent family: _____

Read

5 Reading an Article Read the following article. Then do the exercises.

Changing Families

A   Families in almost every country are changing. This is true in rich countries and poor ones. It is true in Africa, the Americas, Asia, and Europe. All over the world, families are getting smaller.

B   In North Africa, in the past, many people lived in **extended families**. Fifty to a hundred people lived together in a group of houses. These were all   5 family members—grandparents, aunts, uncles, cousins, **children**, and

▲ An extended family

▲ A nuclear family

grandchildren. But now this **traditional family** is breaking into smaller groups.

C   The traditional family in Mexico was also big. One generation ago, the average Mexican woman had seven children. Today, she has an **average** of only 2.5 children. Now, without so many children, families don't need to spend so much money on basics, such as food, clothing, and housing.

D   The traditional Japanese family was also an extended family—a son, his parents, his wife, his children, and his unmarried brothers and sisters. Three generations lived together. But this tradition is changing. Now most families are **nuclear families**—parents and their children—and most Japanese parents have only one or two children. These families have new problems. Many men and women spend a lot of time at work. They don't spend much time together as a family. This can be very difficult. Some young women don't want this kind of **marriage**. They get a job and live with their parents. They say, "I don't need to get **married**."

E   In Europe, in traditional families, the woman stayed home with the children, and the man had a job. But families all over Europe are changing. The number of **divorces** is going up. In Germany, 41 percent of all marriages end in divorce. In Finland, that number is 56 percent. Many Europeans don't get a divorce, but they don't get *married*, either. In much of Europe, many people live alone. In France, more than 26 percent of women between age 30 and 34 live alone, and more than 27 percent of men of the same age live

10

15

20

25

30

35

40

45

Percent of Divorces	
Armenia	18%
Canada	45%
France	43%
Russian Federation	65%
Sweden	64%
Turkey	6%
United States	49%

▲ The number of divorces differs around the world.

alone. The number of **single-parent families** is going up, too. In Denmark, 60 percent of all **first-born** children have parents who are not married. 50

F   The world is changing, and families are changing, too. There are many new types of families, but most seem to be getting smaller. 55

▲ A single-parent family

After You Read

6 **Identifying the Main Ideas** Complete the sentences. Choose the best answer.

1. The main idea is that _____.
   - (A) in North Africa, families are big, but in Europe, they're small
   - (B) families around the world are changing
   - (C) there is more divorce today than in the past

2. The writer thinks that new families are _____.
   - (A) good because they are small
   - (B) different from families in the past
   - (C) bad because people don't live together

UNDERSTANDING PRONOUNS

Pronouns are words such as *he, she, it, they, this, that, these,* or *those.* Pronouns take the place of nouns. Look before the pronoun to find the noun that it replaces. That will help you to understand the pronoun's meaning.

Example My grandfather lived with us. **He** is there in the photo, on the right.
(*He* refers to "My grandfather.")

7 **Understanding Pronouns** Find the meaning of each underlined pronoun. Highlight it. Then draw an arrow from the pronoun to its meaning.

1. Fifty to a hundred people lived together in a group of houses. These were all family members.

2. One generation ago, the average Mexican woman had seven children. Today, she has an average of only 2.5 children.

3. Many men and women spend a lot of time at work. They don't spend much time together as a family.

4. They don't spend much time together as a family. This can be very difficult.

5. Many young women don't want this kind of marriage. <u>They</u> get a job and live with their parents.

6. Many Europeans don't get a divorce, but <u>they</u> don't get *married*, either.

Understanding Organization in an Article or Essay
An essay has a main topic and a main idea. (The topic of the first reading in this chapter is *families*. The main idea is that *families are getting smaller*.) Essays also have subtopics—smaller parts of the main topic. Each subtopic has a main idea, too. Many articles and essays are organized in this way:

> Paragraph A: Introduction of the topic and the main idea of the article or essay

> Paragraph B: Subtopic, main idea, and details

> Paragraph C: Another subtopic, main idea, and details

> Paragraph D: Another subtopic, main idea, and details

> Paragraph E: Another subtopic, main idea, and details

> Paragraph F: Conclusion (restates the main idea of the essay)

8 Understanding Organization in an Essay: Using a Graphic Organizer Fill in this graphic organizer with the topic and the main idea from each paragraph of the reading on pages 42–44. Use your words or copy from the reading.

Paragraph	Topic	Main Idea
A	*families*	*All over the world, families are getting smaller.*
B		
C		*Mexican families are getting smaller.*
D		
E		
F	*families*	

 9 Thinking Critically: Finding Reasons Discuss the following questions. Make a list of possible reasons for each. Then share your answers with the class.

1. Why are families in some countries smaller than in the past?

2. Why are there more single-parent families now?

Our Family Reunion

Before You Read

1 **Making Predictions** Look at the photos in the next essay. Who are these people? What is happening in each picture? What are they saying to each other?

2 **Previewing Vocabulary** Read the words in the list. They are words from the next reading. Listen to their pronunciation. Do not look them up in a dictionary. Check (✓) the words that you know.

Nouns

- ❏ aunts
- ❏ barbecue
- ❏ branches
- ❏ great-grandparents
- ❏ problems
- ❏ relatives
- ❏ reunion
- ❏ team
- ❏ uncles
- ❏ volleyball
- ❏ weddings

Verbs

- ❏ alternate
- ❏ argue
- ❏ drew (draw)

Read

3 **Reading an Essay** Read the following essay. As you read, use the pictures to help with new words. Then do the exercises.

Our Family Reunion

A   These are pictures of my family. I took the pictures last summer. We don't live together. We live in different cities, different states, and two countries. But we often talk to each other on the phone or send email. Every summer all the **relatives** come together for a week. This is our family **reunion,** and it's so much fun.   5

B   There are two **branches** in our family—one branch from Mexico and one from the United States. People come to the reunion from California, Arizona, New York, and Florida. Other people come from Mexico City and Puerto Vallarta. We **alternate** the reunion place—one year in Mexico and the next year in Arizona. My **great-grandparents** lived in Puerto Vallarta,   10 and my grandparents now live in Arizona.

▲ Playing volleyball

C   At the reunion, we have a picnic one day. We play baseball, swim, and eat a lot. We play **volleyball**, too. The women and girls are on one **team**, and the men and boys are on the other. One day some of us go shopping. One night we always have a big **barbecue**. We sit around a fire, tell stories, and eat a lot. Some of my **aunts** and **uncles** sing and play music. On the last night, we have a dinner dance at a nice hotel. We listen to music, dance, and eat a lot. Our family really likes to eat.

D   We don't only eat. We visit with each other all week. We talk about **problems**. We plan **weddings** and cry about divorces. Sometimes we argue. All bring their new babies, new wives and husbands, and new girlfriends and boyfriends.

E   It's good to have a big family. But at the end of the week, I'm always very tired! I'm happy to be alone.

▲ At the barbecue

▲ My cousin's wedding

After You Read

4 **Identifying Main Ideas and Details** Answer the following questions about the story. Choose the best answer.

1. How often does the family have a reunion?
- (A) each month
- (B) every year
- (C) every five years

2. How long is the reunion?
- (A) one week
- (B) two weeks
- (C) one year

3. In the writer's opinion, what's most important about a family reunion?

    (A) It's a chance to eat a lot.

    (B) It brings family members together.

    (C) Everyone brings their new wives or husbands.

4. How does the writer feel at the end of the week?

    (A) unhappy

    (B) hungry

    (C) tired

Culture Note

Friends as "Family"

In many families in the United States and Canada, family members live far from each other—in different cities or states—but their friends live nearby. For some of these people, their friends are very, very important. Their friends are almost a second, new "family." Does this sometimes happen in your country?

USING A DICTIONARY—ALPHABETICAL ORDER

Sometimes you need to use a dictionary. The words in a dictionary are in alphabetical order—A to Z. It's important to know how to alphabetize quickly. You need to look at the first letter of each word to put words in alphabetical order.

Examples

These words are in alphabetical order.

    alcohol

    diet

    food

    walk

If the first letter is the same, you need to look at the second letter, too.

    c**a**ndy

    c**o**uple

    c**u**p

If the first and second letters are the same, you need to look at the third letter, and so on.

    cof**f**ee

    col**a**

    com**p**any

---

5 **Using a Dictionary—Alphabetical Order** Finish writing the 26 letters of the English alphabet in order. Write as fast as you can.

    a   *b*   ____   ____   ____   ____   ____   ____   ____   ____

    ____   ____   ____   ____   ____   ____   ____   ____   ____

    ____   ____   ____   ____   ____   ____

Put the words in alphabetical order by numbering them. The first word is 1; the second word is 2, and so on.

1. _____ every

   _____ elderly

   _____ exercise

   _1_ eggs

2. _____ golf

   _____ gold

   _____ glass

   _____ gray

3. _____ remember

   _____ relatives

   _____ reusable

   _____ reunion

4. _____ full   _____ environment

   _____ marriage   _____ change

   _____ world   _____ fire

5. _____ together   _____ traditional   _____ guy

   _____ visit   _____ group   _____ very

   _____ trees   _____ volleyball   _____ groceries

6. _____ special   _____ cultural   _____ hotel

   _____ almost   _____ reunion   _____ alone

   _____ cry   _____ aunt   _____ come

   _____ husband   _____ safe   _____ shirt

Now go back to the readings that begin on pages 42 and 46. Circle any words that you don't know. Look for them in a dictionary and read their meanings.

6 **Writing in Your Journal** Choose one topic below. Write about it for five minutes. Use some of the vocabulary that you have learned in this chapter.

- how families are changing in your country
- your family
- your own family reunion

Internet Blogs

Reading Tip

Blogs are online journals. People write about their thoughts, their lives. They sometimes put pictures online for family, friends, or other people. People can add comments.

1 Reading a Blog Read Su's blog below. She is from Taiwan and is living in the U.S.

Address http://www.EttyKitt.com

Adventures in a New Country

I was a teacher in Taiwan, but the 5 man I married lives in a small town in New Hampshire, so I came here to be with him. Join me as I learn about the U.S., try to study for graduate school, and adjust to marriage.

Posted by Su | 11:04:53 AM

▲ That's me!

Monday, January 31

Chinese New Year Blues

This will be my first Chinese New Year away from my family. It's 10 hard. When I arrived here in New Hampshire in the summer, I was still very excited about being in a new country, being with my husband, and experiencing all the new sights, sounds, and adventures. Now I have a new thing to be **overwhelmed** by—New Hampshire winter! It's so cold!

I miss all things Chinese. Especially now because it's just a week or so 15 away from Chinese New Year (CNY), which is probably the biggest Chinese cultural celebration anywhere. This town, having an Asian population of just 0.18 percent (that's me and a family that owns a Chinese restaurant), is not the place to be if you're feeling the CNY **blues**.

Here everything is WHITE with snow, while back home in Taiwan 20 everything is RED RED and more RED, Family members that are back home already for the big CNY reunion are helping to decorate the house and maybe even preparing CNY cookies. I miss the color red and my family.

Reading Tip

overwhelmed = very excited

Reading Tip

the blues = sad feelings

Readers talk to Su

Clint said . . .   25

New Year celebrations in Taiwan sound really **cool**. You should post some recipes for traditional CNY food. Then we could all celebrate together. By the way, in what ways is the Chinese calendar different from ours? I'd really like to know.

Christine said . . .   30

You should decorate your house with lots of red! I know it's not the same as being with family, but it would be cool to share it with others!

Melinda said . . .

I know how you feel, Su. I live in France, and there are just some things about my home in Texas that I really miss. For me, it's really hard   35
to be away from home on Thanksgiving. That's my favorite American holiday. I miss a lot of the foods and sights and smells. Although I really want to go back for a visit, I'm happy here. It sounds like you're happy to be where you are, too. :-)

2 **Understanding What You Read** Choose the correct answers below.

1. Su uses CNY as an abbreviation for _____.
   - (A) City of New York
   - (B) Chinese-Americans in New York
   - (C) the Chinese New Year

2. There are _____ in the small town in New Hampshire.
   - (A) a lot of Chinese people
   - (B) very few Chinese people
   - (C) many Asians

3. In Taiwan, Su's family is probably _____.
   - (A) making special cookies
   - (B) celebrating Christmas
   - (C) living in an apartment

4. The color of Chinese New Year's decorations is often _____.
   - (A) blue
   - (B) red
   - (C) we don't know

3 **Adding Comments to the Blog** Write a comment to Su. Then read your comment to a group or a partner.

_____ said . . .

(your name)

_____

_____

_____

USING *GET* AND *HAVE*

The verbs *get* and *have* can be confusing. *Get* is used with some nouns. *Have* is used with other nouns.

1 **Using *Get* and *Have*** Read the sentences below. Write the correct form of the verb *get* or *have* in each blank. You can find the answers in the readings in this chapter.

1. When I _____*have*_____ problems, I talk with my best friend.

2. I don't like my job. I have to go out and _____ a new job.

3. Molly said, "I don't need to _____ married."

4. Most Japanese parents _____ only one or two children.

5. Her parents _____ a divorce when she was 12.

6. Our extended family _____ a family reunion last summer.

7. I would like to _____ a picnic at the next reunion.

2 **Building Vocabulary** Below are words from this chapter. Circle the word that does not belong in each group.

1. wedding   divorce   (average)   marriage

2. reunion   picnic   team   barbecue

3. baseball   team   volleyball   football

4. uncle   aunt   neighbor   relative

5. single-parent   problems   traditional   extended

3 **Focusing on High-Frequency Words** Listen and fill in each blank with a word from the box. Some of the words are new and some of the words are not new. Then check your answers on page 43.

changing	extended	get	much
children	families	marriage	problems

   The traditional Japanese family was also an _____

family—a son, his parents, his wife, his _____, and

his unmarried brothers and sisters. Three generations lived together. But

this tradition is ———————————. Now most ———————————
₃   ₄
are nuclear families—parents and their children—and most Japanese
parents have only one or two children. These families have new
———————————. Many men and women spend a lot of time at
     5
work. They don't spend ——————————— time together as a family.
              6
This can be very difficult. Many young women don't want this kind
of ———————————. They get a job and live with their parents.
   7
They say, "I don't need to ——————————— married."
              8

4 **Writing Sentences with New Vocabulary** Use these words from
Chapter 3 to make your own sentences.

1. traditional / family
The traditional family is changing.

2. percent / divorces
_____

3. family / average
_____

4. children / have
_____

5. use / computer / Internet
_____

5 **Building Vocabulary** Complete the crossword puzzle with words from the box.
These words are from Chapters 1, 2, and 3.

alone	branches	Internet	small
alternate	computer	mall	sold
barbecue	countries	percent	team
blog	customers	red	traditional
blues	divorce	relatives	women

Across

1. examples: children, aunts, uncles, grandfathers, grandmothers (n.)
5. use one, then the other, then the first, then the other again (v.)
8. color of Chinese New Year (adj.)
9. place you go when you go online (n.)
10. group of people playing a sport (n.)
14. journal on a website (n.)
15. what you use to go online (n.)
17. food cooked outside (n.)
18. place with many shops and stores (n.)
19. opposite of *men* (n.)
20. people who buy things (n.)

Down

2. without other people (adv.)
3. past tense of "sell" (v.)
4. parts of a family or of a tree (n.)
6. the same way as in the past (adj.)
7. when marriage ends (n.)
11. nations, such as Japan, Mexico, and China (n.)
12. sad feelings (n.)
13. opposite of *large* (adj.)
16. % (n.)

KEY: *adj.* = adjective; *adv.* = adverb; *n.* = noun; *prep.* = preposition; *v.* = verb

Self-Assessment Log

Read the lists below. Check (✓) the strategies and vocabulary that you know. Look through the chapter or ask your instructor about the other strategies and words.

Reading and Vocabulary-Building Strategies

- ❏ Previewing vocabulary
- ❏ Skimming
- ❏ Understanding new words: using pictures
- ❏ Identifying the main ideas and details
- ❏ Understanding pronouns
- ❏ Understanding organization in an essay: using a graphic organizer
- ❏ Predicting
- ❏ Using a dictionary—alphabetical order
- ❏ Using *get* and *have*
- ❏ Reading an Internet blog
- ❏ Writing sentences with new vocabulary

Target Vocabulary

Nouns

- ❏ aunts
- ❏ average*
- ❏ barbecue
- ❏ blog
- ❏ the blues
- ❏ branches*
- ❏ children (child)*
- ❏ divorces
- ❏ extended families
- ❏ families (family)*
- ❏ marriage*
- ❏ nuclear families
- ❏ problems*
- ❏ relatives*
- ❏ reunion
- ❏ single-parent families
- ❏ team
- ❏ traditional family
- ❏ uncles
- ❏ volleyball
- ❏ weddings
- ❏ women (woman)*

Verbs

- ❏ alternate
- ❏ changing*
- ❏ get*
- ❏ have

Adjectives

- ❏ extended* (family)
- ❏ first-born
- ❏ married*
- ❏ much*

*These words are among the 1,000 most-frequently used words in English.

Health Care

Are you healthy? In this chapter, you will read about ways to stay healthy. In Part 1, you will read about foods, drinks, and lifestyles that will help you stay healthy. Both physical and mental health will be discussed. You will fill out a short questionnaire in Part 2 that will help you to answer the question, "Am I healthy?" In Part 3, you will learn language about the body, illnesses, and going to the doctor. In Part 4, you will have a chance to practice new vocabulary.

" Prevention is better than cure. **"**

—Desiderius Erasmus
Dutch humanist and theologian (1466–1536)

Connecting to the Topic

1 What is the woman doing? What are the other people doing?

2 Why are they doing these things? Are these things healthy?

3 What are five healthy things that people do? What are five unhealthy things?

Health News for Body and Mind

1 Thinking About the Topic Look at this chart. Which things are good for your health? Which are bad? Check (✓) *Good* or *Bad* in one of the first two columns.

Then make another decision. Are they good for your physical health (your body) or your mental health? Check (✓) *Physical Health, Mental Health*, both, or neither.

Good	Bad	Item		Good for Physical Health	Good for Mental Health
		fruit			
		vegetables			
		exercise			
		water			
		sugar			
		chocolate			
		problems and worry			
		sleep			

2 **Comparing Answers** Show your chart to other students. Are your answers the same? Which answers are different?

3 **Previewing Vocabulary** Read the words in the list. They are words from the next reading. Listen to their pronunciation. Do not look them up in a dictionary. Check (✓) the words that you know.

Nouns
- ❑ antioxidants
- ❑ beverages
- ❑ blood pressure
- ❑ body
- ❑ brain
- ❑ calcium
- ❑ cocoa
- ❑ couch potato
- ❑ diseases

- ❑ DNA
- ❑ junk food
- ❑ sleep
- ❑ stress
- ❑ university
- ❑ wrinkles

Verbs
- ❑ age
- ❑ damage
- ❑ exercise

- ❑ sleep
- ❑ smoke
- ❑ solves

Adjectives
- ❑ bilingual
- ❑ chronic
- ❑ difficult
- ❑ healthy
- ❑ mental
- ❑ physical

- ❑ sleep-deprived
- ❑ surprising

Adverb
- ❑ often

Strategy

Finding Meaning After *Which* or *Who*
You do not always need to use a dictionary to find the meaning of a new word. Sometimes the meaning of a new word comes after a comma and the word *which* or *who*.

Example

Too much **stress**, which is worry about problems in life, is not good for health.

A **dentist**, who takes care of people's teeth, has an interesting profession.

---

4 **Finding Meaning After *Which* or *Who*** The meanings of these words are in the next reading. Find the words and circle their meanings.

chronic	sleep-deprived	bilingual

Read

5 **Reading an Article** Read the following article. Don't use your dictionary. If you don't know some words, try to figure out their meanings. Then do the exercises.

Health News for Body and Mind

A   Nobody wants to be **sick**. Everyone wants to be **healthy**, and most people want to have a long life, too. But a healthy **body** is not enough. We all want both **physical** and **mental** health. What can we do to stay well? Most of us know some things to do. It's a good idea to **exercise** (for example, in a gym), eat fruit, vegetables, and fish, and drink lots of water. We also 5 know things *not* to do; it's a bad idea to eat a lot of **junk food**, such as chips, ice cream, candy, donuts, and other foods with sugar or fat. It's a bad idea to be a **couch potato**—a person who watches a lot of TV and doesn't exercise. It's a terrible idea to **smoke**. But scientists now have new information about *other* ways to stay healthy. Some of it is **surprising**. 10

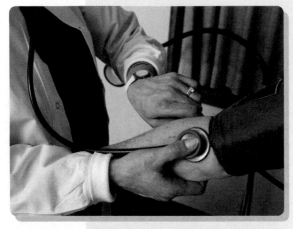

▲ High blood pressure is bad for health. (Normal blood pressure is 120/80.)

▲ Gray hair and wrinkles are natural effects of aging.

▲ A model of DNA

Drink Cocoa

B   Several **beverages** are good for the health. Orange juice has vitamin C. Milk has **calcium**. Black tea and green tea are good for health, too. They have **antioxidants**; these fight **diseases** such as cancer and heart disease. 15 Most people know this. But most people *don't* know about **cocoa**—hot chocolate. They enjoy the sweet, chocolaty beverage, but they don't know about its antioxidants. It has more antioxidants than tea! 20

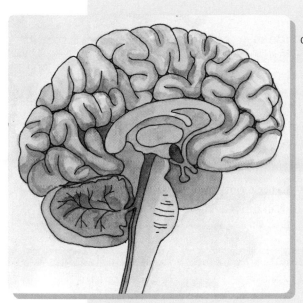
▲ The brain **solves** problems.

Relax

C   Too much **stress**, which is worry about problems in life, is not good for physical health. For example, it makes your **blood pressure** go up. Now we know more. Some stress is **chronic**, which means that it lasts a long time—for many months or years. Chronic stress can make people old. As people get older, they get gray hair and **wrinkles** in their skin, and their eyesight and hearing become worse. This is normal. But chronic stress makes people **age**—grow old—*faster*. A scientist at the University of California, San Francisco, studies stress. She can now identify *how* stress makes people age. It can **damage** (hurt) the body's **DNA**. The lesson from this is clear. We need to learn to relax.

Sleep

D   One easy and cheap way to help both your physical and mental health is just to sleep eight hours or more every night, but more and more people are not sleeping enough. According to the World Health Organization, over half the people in the world may be **sleep-deprived**, which means they don't get enough sleep. Sleep-deprived people often have medical problems, such as high blood pressure, diabetes (a problem with sugar in the blood), and heart problems. It is also more **difficult** for them to make decisions. Clearly, we need to find time to get more sleep. But there is another reason. A new study from Germany found that sleep makes people *smarter*. The study shows that the **brain** continues to work during sleep and helps the sleeper to work on problems. You didn't do your homework last night? Maybe you can tell your teacher that you were working hard in your sleep!

Learn Languages

E   How many languages do you speak? There might be good news for you. A study from **a university** in Canada found something interesting. **Bilingual** people, who speak two languages very well, do better on tests than people who speak only one language. It seems to be mental "exercise" to hold two languages in your brain. Ellen Bialystock of York University says it's "like going to a brain gym."

Conclusion

F   To have good physical and mental health, we need to eat right, relax, sleep enough, and exercise (both the body and the brain). There is a lot of new information about health. Some of it is surprising. We need to know about it.

After You Read

6 **Understanding the Main Ideas** According to the reading, what is good for your health? Write *G* for *Good*. What is bad for your health? Write *B* for *Bad*.

1. _____ cocoa

2. _____ stress

3. _____ sleep

4. _____ speaking two languages

7 **Identifying Vocabulary** Write the word or term for the meanings below. For help, look back at the boldfaced words in the reading.

	Meaning	Word or Term
1.	person who watches a lot of TV and doesn't exercise	*couch potato*
2.	examples: chips, ice cream, candy, donuts, and other foods with sugar or fat	
3.	something in milk that is good for the health	
4.	example: cancer	
5.	problems and worry about your life	
6.	lasting a long time (months or years)	
7.	get old	
8.	without enough sleep	
9.	speaking two languages	

8 **Finding Important Details** Work with classmates to fill in a chart like this with information from Paragraphs B–E. How many details can you find?

What is good for your health?	Why?
orange juice	*It has vitamin C.*
What is bad for your health?	**Why?**

9 **Understanding Pronouns** Find and highlight the meaning of each underlined pronoun. Then draw an arrow from the pronoun to its meaning.

1. Many people don't know about cocoa. <u>It</u> has more antioxidants than tea.

2. They have antioxidants; <u>these</u> fight diseases.

3. Some stress is chronic, which means <u>it</u> lasts a long time.

4. A scientist at the University of California studies stress. <u>She</u> can now identify how stress makes people age.

5. Green tea and black tea are good for the health. <u>They</u> have antioxidants.

Strategy

Understanding Italics

Italics are slanted letters, *like these.* Writers use them for different reasons. One reason is for words that are important. When people read out loud, these words sound a little louder and higher than other words.

---

 10 **Understanding Italics** Go back to the reading. How many words can you find in italics? Read those sentences out loud to a partner.

CHANGING NOUNS TO ADJECTIVES

Sometimes we can change a noun to an adjective by adding a *-y* to the singular form of the noun. For example, to change the noun *health* into an adjective, we add a *-y*. *Healthy* means "in good health."

> **Example**
> She's in good **health**. (noun)
> She's a **healthy** person. (adjective)

If the noun ends in a vowel, you have to drop the vowel before adding *-y.*
> **Example**
> I love **chocolate**. (noun)
> I love this **chocolaty** dessert. (adjective)

---

11 **Changing Nouns to Adjectives** Complete the following sentences with the appropriate adjective. Change a noun in the sentence to an adjective.

1. If a person is very smart (has a good *brain*), she is _____*brainy*_____.

2. If you have a lot of luck, you are _____.

3. If something has a lot of dirt, it's _____.

4. If you need sleep, you are _____.

5. A drink is cold because it has ice in it. It is an _____ drink.

 12 **Discussing the Reading** Discuss the following questions.

1. According to new studies, what diseases can cocoa fight?

2. What can you do to get old more slowly?

3. What can you do to be smarter?

Are You Healthy?

Before You Read

1 Making Predictions Before you do the questionnaire in the next activity, answer this question:

How is your health? Check (✓) one.

_____ great _____ good _____ okay _____ bad _____ terrible

2 Previewing Vocabulary Read the words in the list. They are words from the next reading. Listen to their pronunciation. Do not look them up in a dictionary. Check (✓) the words that you know.

Nouns	Adjective	Adverbs
❑ alcohol	❑ overweight	❑ never
❑ breakfast		❑ seldom
❑ cigarettes		❑ sometimes
❑ pounds		❑ usually

Read

3 Reading and Answering a Questionnaire Read the questions in this questionnaire. Choose your answers. This will help you to answer the question, "Am I healthy?"

Am I Healthy?

1. Do you eat a healthful breakfast every day?
   - (A) yes
   - (B) usually
   - (C) no
2. Do you eat fruits and vegetables every day?
   - (A) yes, 5 or more
   - (B) yes, 1 or 2
   - (C) no

3. Do you smoke?
   - (A) never
   - (B) yes, 1–10 cigarettes every day
   - (C) yes, more than 10 cigarettes every day

4. Do you drink cola?
   - (A) no
   - (B) yes, 1–2 glasses every day
   - (C) yes, 3–10 glasses every day

5. Do you eat junk food?
   - (A) never
   - (B) sometimes
   - (C) often

▲ Do you eat junk food?

6. How much do you sleep every night?
   - (A) 8–9 hours
   - (B) 6–7 hours
   - (C) 3–5 hours

7. Are you overweight?
   - (A) no
   - (B) yes, 5–19 pounds
   - (C) yes, 20–50 pounds

8. How much stress do you have?
   - (A) very little
   - (B) some
   - (C) a lot, every day

9. How far do you walk every day?
   - (A) 1–5 miles
   - (B) $\frac{1}{2}$–1 mile
   - (C) 0 miles

10. How often do you exercise?
    - (A) often
    - (B) 1 time every week
    - (C) seldom or never

11. How much alcohol (beverages like beer and wine) do you drink every week?
    - (A) 0–7 glasses
    - (B) 8–12 glasses
    - (C) 13 or more glasses

12. Do you worry, or are you unhappy?
    - (A) seldom
    - (B) sometimes
    - (C) often

Next, add up your score.

> Every answer *a* = 3 points.
> Every answer *b* = 2 points.
> Every answer *c* = 0 points.

YOUR SCORE: _____

Am I healthy?

> 30–36 points = You're probably very healthy.
> 25–29 points = You might need to make some changes.
> 0–24 points = You might not be very healthy.

Culture Note

Smoking

In some countries, people are trying to stop smoking. In other countries, more people (especially young people) are beginning to smoke. What is the situation where you live? What is the situation in another country that you know well?

After You Read

GIVING ADVICE

To give another person advice, you can use the modal *should*.

should ┐
        ├── + the simple form of the verb
should not ┘

Example

You **shouldn't worry** so much. You **should try** to relax.

4 Discussing the Reading: Giving Advice Work with a partner. Look at your partner's answers to the questions on the health test. Give your partner advice. Use *should* and *shouldn't*.

Example

You should eat a good breakfast every day.

Using a Dictionary—Guide Words

Sometimes you can't understand a new word without a dictionary. If you want to find a word fast, you need to use guide words. Guide words are at the top of every dictionary page, usually in the left and right corners.

Example

Look at the dictionary page below. The guide words are *picnic* and *pig*. The first word on this page is *picnic*. The last word is *pig*. The words are in alphabetical order between these two guide words. Look at the guide words, and you'll know if your new word is on this page.

picnic	386	pig

picnic (4) [pik'nik], *n.* a meal planned for eating outdoors. **Ex.** *They ate their picnic beside the river.* —*v.* have a picnic. **Ex.** *We picnicked in the woods.* —**pic'nick·er**, *n.* **Ex.** *After lunch, the picnickers made up teams for a game of baseball.*

picture (1) [pik'čər], *n.* 1. a painting, drawing, or photograph. **Ex.** *That picture of the President is seen often in the newspaper.* 2. that which strongly resembles another; an image. **Ex.** *She is the picture of her mother.* 3. a description. **Ex.** *The author gives a lively picture of his life as a sailor.* 4. a motion picture; movie. **Ex.** *The whole family enjoyed the picture we saw last night.* —*v.* describe. **Ex.** *The speaker pictured the scene in colorful words.* —**pic·tor'i·al**, *adj.*

pie (2) [pay'], *n.* a baked dish consisting of a thin shell, and sometimes a cover, made of flour and cooking oil and filled with fruit, meat, etc. **Ex.** *She put the pie in the oven to bake.*

piece (1) [piys'], *n.* 1. an amount or a part considered as an individual unit. **Ex.** *Please give me a piece of writing paper.* 2. a part taken away from something larger. **Ex.** *She cut the pie into six pieces.* 3. a coin. **Ex.** *Can you change this fifty-cent piece?* —*v.* join together; make whole. **Ex.** *She pieced together the broken dish.* —**go to pieces,** become upset or excited. **Ex.** *He goes to pieces when I disagree with him.*

piecemeal [piys'miyl`], *adv.* one part at a time; piece by piece. **Ex.** *He put the machine together piecemeal in his spare time.*

piecework [piys'wərk`], *n.* work paid for by the piece finished instead of by the hour, day, etc. **Ex.** *She does piecework at home.*

pier (3) [pi:r'], *n.* a structure built over the water and used as a landing place for ships and boats. **Ex.** *The ship is at pier seven.*

pierce (4) [pirs'], *v.* 1. break into or through. **Ex.** *The knife had pierced the wall.* 2. make a hole or opening in. **Ex.** *Many girls have their ears pierced for earrings.* 3. force a way through. **Ex.** *They tried to pierce the enemy's defense.* 4. deeply or sharply affect the senses or feelings. **Ex.** *They were pierced by the icy winds.*

pig (2) [pig'], *n.* a farm animal with a broad nose and fat body, raised for its meat.

PIG

5 **Using a Dictionary—Guide Words** Use your dictionary. Find the following pages quickly. What are the guide words? Write them on the blanks. If there are no guide words, write the first and last words on the page.

1. page 32 _____ _____

2. page 196 _____ _____

3. page 15 _____ _____

4. page 203 _____ _____

5. page 78 _____ _____

6 **Understanding Guide Words** Read the vocabulary words and the guide words below. For each number answer this question: *Could you find this vocabulary word between the guide words?* Write *yes* or *no* on each line below.

Vocabulary Words	Guide Words
1. _no_ speak	sleep–smoke
2. ____ beverage	bed–big
3. ____ new	never–night
4. ____ mental	most–mother
5. ____ overweight	old–pitcher
6. ____ damage	dance–difficult
7. ____ solve	sick–sometimes
8. ____ wrinkle	walk–weight

7 **Using a Dictionary** Find these words in your dictionary. Use the guide words in the dictionary for help. Write the page number and the guide words for each word.

Word	Page	Guide Words	Word	Page	Guide Words
elbow			cough		
headache			throat		
stomach			thumb		
pain			cold		

8 **Writing in Your Journal** Choose one topic below. Write about it for five minutes. Use some of the vocabulary that you have learned in this chapter.

- things that you do that are good for your health
- something that you do that is not good for your health
- something that you learned about health in this chapter

Going to the Doctor

1 **Identifying Body Parts** Read the body parts in the box. Then read the sentences and look at the picture. Write the body part in each blank and next to the correct number in the picture.

ankle	elbow	head	nose
chest	eyes	hip	shoulder
chin	fingers	knee	toes
ears	foot	neck	wrist

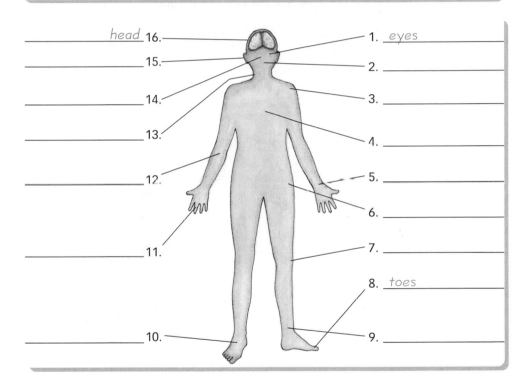

head 16.

15.

14.

13.

12.

11.

10.

1. _eyes_

2.

3.

4.

5.

6.

7.

8. _toes_

9.

1. You use me to see. I'm your _____ _eyes_ _____.

2. I'm below your mouth. I'm your _____.

3. I'm between your neck and your arm. I'm your _____.

4. I'm the part of your body where your heart is. I'm your _____.

5. I connect your hand and your arm. I'm your _____.

6. I connect your leg to your body. I'm your _____.

7. I'm in the middle of your leg. I'm your _____.

8. There are ten of me—five on each foot. I'm your _____ *toes* _____.

9. I connect your foot and your leg. I'm your _____.

10. Five toes are on me. I'm your _____.

11. You have ten of me on your hands, and they help you write. I'm your _____.

12. I'm in the middle of your arm. I'm your _____.

13. I connect your head to your body. I'm your _____.

14. I smell things. I'm your _____.

15. I hear things. I'm your _____.

16. Your ears are on my right and left sides. I'm your _____ *head* _____.

2 **Identifying Body Parts: Inside** Look at the picture of the body. Then look at the words in the box. Write the names of the body parts on the blank lines. If you don't know the names, you can look in a dictionary.

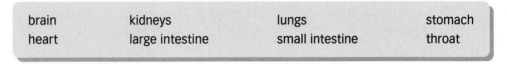

brain	kidneys	lungs	stomach
heart	large intestine	small intestine	throat

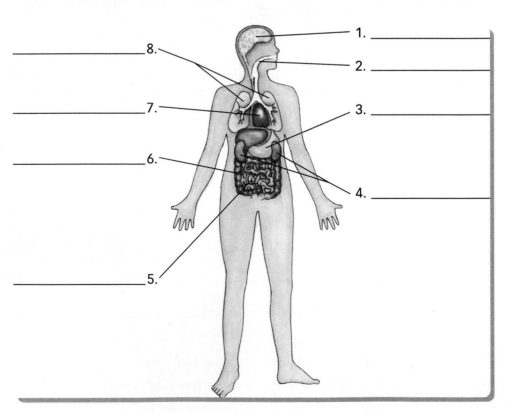

DESCRIBING ILLNESSES

Sometimes people get sick. Here are some illnesses that people sometimes have.

a headache.

a stomachache.

I have ——— a cough.

a pain in my arm.

a cold.

---

3 **Describing Illnesses** Look at the photo below. What do you think the people are saying? Work with a partner and create a short conversation. The doctor can ask questions like these: "How are you feeling?" or "What's wrong?" The patient can answer by completing this sentence: "I have _____."

▲ "How are you feeling?"

4 **Matching Meaning** We use the word *heart* in many expressions in English. Can you guess the meaning of the expressions below?

1. ___c___ The museum is right *in the heart of* the new downtown.

   a. He is very sad.

2. _____ His wife asked for a divorce. *His heart is breaking.*

   b. a problem with your heart

3. _____ *A heart attack* is a very serious medical emergency.

   c. in the middle of

4. _____ She never liked fish before, but now she loves fish. She had *a change of heart* about fish.

   d. the way she feels inside, not the way she looks on the outside

5. _____ I love you. You *make my heart sing.*

   e. in your true feelings

6. _____ He doesn't like anyone. He *has a cold heart.*

   f. give me happiness

7. _____ In this argument, *in your heart of hearts,* you know I'm right.

   g. is mean

8. _____ My grandmother loves to play with children. She's really a kid *at heart.*

   h. a new feeling or idea

Part 4   Vocabulary Practice

1 **Building Vocabulary** Read the words below. Which word does not fit? Circle it.

1.	beverage	tea	cocoa	(blood)
2.	headache	pain	healthy	disease
3.	brain	foot	kidneys	heart
4.	pounds	usually	overweight	food
5.	sometimes	chronic	seldom	never
6.	alcohol	drink	eat	wine
7.	never	usually	often	daily
8.	lungs	cigarettes	sleep	smoke
9.	stomachache	wrinkle	physical	sick

2 **Identifying Opposites** Draw a line to the word that has the opposite meaning.

1. small   **a.** old

2. healthy   **b.** relaxation

3. new   **c.** underweight

4. overweight   **d.** wake

5. stress   **e.** kindergarten

6. never   **f.** easy

7. breakfast   **g.** sick

8. university   **h.** large

9. mental   **i.** physical

10. difficult   **j.** always

11. sleep   **k.** dinner

3 **Focusing on High-Frequency Words: Listening** Listen and fill in the words from the reading on page 61. Then check your work.

How many _____ do you speak? There might be good news for
                        1

you. A study from a _____ in Canada found something interesting.
                          2

_____ people, who speak two languages very well, do better on
    3

tests than people who _____ only one language. It seems to be
                              4

_____ "exercise" to hold two languages in your brain. Ellen
    5

Bialystock of York University says it's "like going to a _____ gym."
                                                              6

To have good physical and mental health, we need to _____
                                                          7

right, relax, _____ enough, and _____ (both the
              8   9

_____ and the brain). There is a lot of new information about
    8

health. Some of it is _____. We need to know about it.
                      11

4 **Building Vocabulary** Complete the crossword puzzle. These words are from Chapter 4.

age	chin	damage	intestine
beverages	chronic	diseases	junk food
chest	cocoa	healthy	kidneys
mental	sick	stomach	wrinkles
never	solve	stress	

Across

4. worry (n.)
6. hurt, harm, or break something (v.)
9. lines on your skin (n.)
11. drinks of all kinds (n.)
12. Your heart is inside this. (n.)
16. unhealthful things to eat (two words) (n.)
18. always there; lasting a long time (adj.)
19. When you do this to a problem, the problem is fixed. (v.)

Down

1. cancer, AIDS, heart problems, diabetes (n.)
2. not even once (adv.)
3. opposite of sick (adj.)
5. opposite of healthy (adj.)
7. get older (v.)
8. You have both a large and a small one of these. (n.)
10. a hot chocolate drink (n.)
13. where your food goes first when you eat (n.)
14. There are two of these, on the right and left, near your stomach. (n.)
15. happening in the mind (adj.)
17. This is below your mouth. (n.)

KEY: *adj.* = adjective; *adv.* = adverb; *n.* = noun; *prep.* = preposition; *v.* = verb

Self-Assessment Log

Read the lists below. Check (✓) the strategies and vocabulary that you know. Look through the chapter or ask your instructor about the other strategies and words.

Reading and Vocabulary-Building Strategies

❑ Finding meaning after *which* or *who*
❑ Identifying vocabulary
❑ Finding important details
❑ Understanding pronouns
❑ Understanding italics
❑ Changing nouns to adjectives
❑ Giving advice
❑ Using a dictionary: understanding guide words
❑ Identifying body parts
❑ Describing illnesses
❑ Identifying opposites

Target Vocabulary

Nouns

❑ alcohol
❑ ankle
❑ beverages
❑ blood*
❑ body*
❑ brain
❑ breakfast
❑ calcium
❑ chest
❑ chin
❑ cigarettes
❑ cocoa
❑ couch potato
❑ cough
❑ diseases
❑ ears*
❑ elbow
❑ eyes*
❑ fingers
❑ foot
❑ head*
❑ heart*

❑ hip
❑ junk food
❑ kidneys
❑ knee
❑ large intestine
❑ lungs
❑ mouth*
❑ neck
❑ nose
❑ pounds*
❑ shoulder*
❑ sleep*
❑ small intestine
❑ stomach
❑ stress
❑ throat
❑ thumb
❑ toes
❑ university*
❑ wrinkles
❑ wrist

Verbs

❑ age*
❑ damage
❑ exercise*
❑ should
❑ sleep*
❑ smoke
❑ solves

Adjectives

❑ bilingual
❑ chronic
❑ difficult*
❑ healthy
❑ mental
❑ overweight
❑ physical
❑ sleep-deprived
❑ surprising*

Adverbs

❑ never*
❑ often*
❑ seldom
❑ sometimes*
❑ usually*

---

*These words are among the 1,000 most-frequently used words in English.

Men and Women

In This Chapter

You will read about differences between men's and women's styles of conversation. Who do you think talks more, men or women? What do men say about women? What do women say about men? You'll find the answers to these questions in Parts 1 and 2. In Part 3, you will learn how certain words include or exclude men and women. Part 4 then provides additional opportunities to practice vocabulary.

❝ Women marry men hoping they will change. Men marry women hoping they will not. So each is inevitably disappointed. ❞

—Albert Einstein
German-born American physicist (1879–1955)

Connecting to the Topic

1 What is their relationship to each other? What are they talking about?

2 What is each person feeling? What happened just before this photo?

3 What are five issues that couples or roommates have to discuss when they live together?

Men's Talk and Women's Talk in the United States

Before You Read

1 Interviewing Other Students Look at the chart below. Walk around the room and ask as many students as possible the two questions. Write their answers in this chart. For Question 1, use symbols to show the number of people who gave each answer. For example, || = 2 people, |||| = 5 people. For question 2, write your classmates' answers in words.

Question 1	Men's Answers		Women's Answers	
	Men talk more.	Women talk more.	Men talk more.	Women talk more.
Who talks more—men or women?				

Question 2	Men's Answers	Women's Answers
What topics do you like to talk about with your friends or family?		

2 Thinking Critically: Understanding Humor Read the cartoons on the next page. Then discuss the following questions.

1. In Cartoon 1, the man doesn't understand something. What is it?

2. In Cartoon 1, the woman is a little angry. Why? What does she want?

3. In Cartoon 2, the woman is unhappy. Why? What does she want?

4. In Cartoon 2, the man is unhappy. Why? What does he want?

5. Do men and women talk in different ways? Give examples.

▲ Cartoon 1

▲ Cartoon 2

3 **Previewing Vocabulary** Read the words in the list. They are words from the next reading. Listen to their pronunciation. Do not look them up in a dictionary. Check (✓) the words that you know.

Nouns	Verbs	Adjectives	Preposition
❏ conversations	❏ apologize	❏ active	❏ according to
❏ feelings	❏ argue	❏ close	
❏ hierarchy	❏ brag	❏ equal	
❏ orders	❏ socialize	❏ private	
❏ position		❏ public	
❏ suggestions		❏ similar	

Strategy

Understanding New Words in a Reading
You do not always need to use a dictionary to find the meaning of a new word. Sometimes the meaning is in the sentence before or after the word.

Example
I apologized to my friend. I said, "I'm really sorry about yesterday."
(*Apologize* means to say you're sorry about something.)

Sometimes the meaning is after the phrase *in other words*.

Example
He has a low place in the hierarchy, **in other words,** the system from low to high.
(*Hierarchy* means the system from low to high.)

4 **Understanding New Words in a Reading** The meanings of these words are in the next article. Find the words and underline their meanings.

similar	brag	equal	private
orders	suggestions	active	public

Read

5 **Reading an Article** Read the following article. Don't use your dictionary. If you don't know some words, try to figure out their meaning. (See the Strategy Box above.) Then do the exercises.

Men's Talk and Women's Talk in the United States

A   Marriage is often not easy. Love is often not easy. Sometimes friendship between a man and a woman is not easy. Maybe a man and a woman love or like each other, but they **argue**. They get angry. Later they **apologize**, but it happens again and again. What's the problem? Are men and women really very different?

B   Deborah Tannen says yes, men and women are very different. Tannen teaches at Georgetown University in Washington, D.C. She writes books about the ways people talk. She believes that men and women talk—and think—in different ways. She tells about some differences in her book, *You Just Don't Understand*.

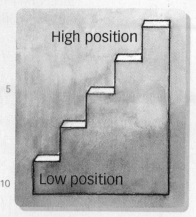
▲ A hierarchy is the system from low to high.

It Begins in Childhood

C   The differences, Tannen says, begin when men and women are children. Very young boys and girls are **similar** to each other. In other words, they like many of the same things and play in the same ways. They aren't very different. But then there is a change. When children in the United States are five or six years old, boys usually play in large groups. One boy gives **orders**. For example, he says, "Take this," "Go over there," and "Be on this team." He is the leader. Boys also **brag**. In other words, they say good things about themselves. They do this to have a high **position**—place—in the **hierarchy**, in other words, the system from low to high. Position in the group is important to boys.

▲ Equal positions in the hierarchy

D   Girls in the United States usually play in small groups or with one other girl. A girl's "best friend"—her very, very good friend—is important to her. Girls don't often give orders; they give **suggestions**. For example, they say, "Let's go over there," "Maybe we should do this," and "Do you want to play with that?" Girls don't usually have a leader, and they don't often brag. Everyone has an **equal** position. 40

E   Boys and girls play in different ways, too. Much of the time, little girls sit together and *talk*. They have conversations. Little boys are usually **active**; they *do* things. When children grow up, nothing really changes.

Who Talks More, and Why?

F   Many people believe that women talk more than men do. **According to** 45 Deborah Tannen, this isn't exactly true. She says women talk more than men only in **private** situations—at home, with family, or with a few friends. In **public** situations—in other words, in a big group or at work, *men* talk more. Tannen says that men and women often talk for different reasons. Men talk to give or get information. They also talk to get or keep a 50 high position among other men. But for women, people and **feelings** are important. Women often talk to **socialize** and show interest and love. They also talk to keep their **close** relationships with friends and family.

Conclusion

G   Although a man and a woman might speak the same language, sometimes they don't understand each other. Men's talk and women's talk 55 are almost two different languages. But maybe men and women can learn to understand each other if they understand the differences in speech.

After You Read

6 Identifying the Main Ideas and Details Read the sentences below. Check (✓) Men or Women for each sentence. You can find the information in the reading.

	Men	Women
1. As children, they play in small groups or with one best friend.		
2. As children, they play in large groups.		
3. High position is important to them.		
4. They want everyone in a group to have a similar position.		
5. They often talk to show interest and love.		
6. They often talk to give and get information.		
7. They talk more in private situations.		
8. They talk more in public situations.		

7 Checking Vocabulary Write the words for the meanings below. For help, look back at the boldfaced words in paragraphs C, D, and F of the reading.

	Meaning	Word
1.	commands such as "Take this," or "Go over there."	
2.	with the same position	
3.	*doing* things	
4.	ideas about what to do	
5.	almost the same	
6.	say good things about themselves	
7.	in a big group or at work	
8.	at home, with family, or with a few friends	

8 Identifying a Good Summary Read the summaries below. Which is a good summary of the article "Men's Talk and Women's Talk in the United States"? Why is it good? Why are the others not good? Compare your answer with a partner's.

a. Marriage is not easy. Men and women may argue. They may apologize later. This problem can happen many times. Men and women can learn to understand each other if they listen to each other.

b. Men and women talk and think differently. These differences begin as children. Men often talk to give or get information. Women often talk to show interest and love. These differences can cause problems.

c. Deborah Tannen teaches at Georgetown University. She is a writer. She writes about how people talk. She says that men and women are different. She wrote a book called *You Just Don't Understand*.

 9 Discussing the Reading Talk about your answers to the following questions.

1. When you were a child, did you play in a big group or a small group? Did you have a best friend?

2. What are the benefits of having a high position in a group? A low position? An equal position?

3. What do (or did) you sometimes argue about with your husband? Wife? Boyfriend? Girlfriend?

4. The article is about the United States. Is the situation in other countries similar or different? For example, do men talk to women the same way as they talk to other men? Do women talk to other women differently than they talk to men? Do women and men act differently? Do women and men work at different jobs?

He Said/She Said: A U.S. Couple

Before You Read

1 Making Predictions Look at the pictures in the next reading. Where are the man and woman? Who are they talking to? What are they talking about?

2 Previewing Vocabulary Read the words in the list. They are words from the next reading. Listen to their pronunciation. Do not look them up in a dictionary. Check (✓) the words that you know.

Noun	**Verb**	**Adjectives**	**Adverb**
❑ politics	❑ fix	❑ lonely	❑ full time
		❑ unimportant	
		❑ uninteresting	

Read

3 Reading Two Views About the Same Thing Read these two paragraphs about the same marriage. One is the husband's view, and the other is the wife's view.

He Said/She Said: A U.S. Couple

A   **W**ell, Doctor, I'm beginning to worry about my marriage. My wife and I just don't understand each other. She doesn't like to do things with me. She won't play tennis or baseball ₅ with me. She doesn't like to **fix** the car with me. She doesn't work on the house with me—you know, paint the house or fix the roof. She doesn't listen when I talk about interesting things: ₁₀ sports, money, or world **politics**. Sometimes she gets angry with me about **unimportant** things. And she talks and talks and talks about **uninteresting** things. What's wrong with her?

▲ "We just don't understand each other."

B   Well, Doctor, I'm beginning to worry about my marriage. My husband and I 15 just don't understand each other. We both work **full time**, but I do all the work at home—you know, fix dinner, wash clothes, and clean the house. His life is easy; he has only one job. I have 20 two! Sometimes I feel so **lonely**. When he's home, he reads the newspaper or watches TV. He doesn't talk with me; he

▲ "I'm beginning to worry about my marriage."

talks *at* me. He only talks with his friends. He doesn't listen if I tell him about my day. He isn't interested in our friends and relatives. Sometimes he 25 gives me orders. Sometimes he tells me about sports or politics, but I don't like it because I feel like a student in school. What's wrong with him?

Culture Note

Marriage Problems

Sometimes American couples go to a marriage counselor for help with their marriage. Does this happen in other cultures that you know about? Is it common? If not, what do people do about marriage problems?

After You Read

4 Identifying the Main Idea What is the main idea of the reading?

- (A) The man is unhappy because his wife doesn't like to do things, such as fixing the car with him.
- (B) The wife is unhappy because her husband doesn't talk with her and doesn't listen to her.
- (C) The husband and wife have problems with their marriage because they communicate in different ways.

5 Identifying Details Read the article again. Then answer the two questions below. You may check (✓) more than one answer for each question.

1. The man in the article is unhappy about many things. What does he say?
   a. _____ His wife doesn't like to do things with him.
   b. _____ His wife talks about uninteresting things.
   c. _____ His wife gives him orders.
   d. _____ His wife doesn't listen when he talks about sports, money, or politics.

2. The woman is also unhappy about many things. What does she say?
   a. _____ Her husband gets angry about unimportant things.
   b. _____ She goes to work and does all the work at home, too.
   c. _____ Her husband doesn't talk with her.
   d. _____ Her husband gives her orders.

Strategy

Reading Faster

Students usually need to read fast because they have to read many books each year. Also, they can understand more if they read fast. One way to read faster is to read groups of words, or phrases, not one word at a time. Look at the example. Then do the exercise.

Example

Slow readers read one word at a time, like this.

Fast readers usually read words in phrases, like this. This helps them to understand more.

6 Practicing Reading in Phrases Read the following sentences in phrases (groups of words). Read silently; in other words, do not speak.

Men and women sometimes seem to speak different languages. They like to talk about different things. Sometimes they don't listen to each other. A woman makes a suggestion, but her husband doesn't understand. A man tries to help, but his wife doesn't like it. Maybe they should go to language school!

Now read the paragraph. Focus on the phrases, not the separate words:

> Men and women sometimes seem to speak different languages. They like to talk about different things. Sometimes they don't listen to each other. A woman makes a suggestion, but her husband doesn't understand. A man tries to help, but his wife doesn't like it. Maybe they should go to language school!

7 Discussing the Reading Talk about your answers to the following questions.

1. Are people in other countries similar to or different from the man and woman in the reading on pages 84–85? In other words, do they say similar things about each other?

2. Choose a country that you know well. List some things about the people there that are different from the couple in the reading. List some things that are similar.

8 Writing in Your Journal Choose one topic below. Write about it for five minutes. Use some of the vocabulary that you have learned in this chapter.

- something that you learned about men's and women's conversation
- things that you like to talk about
- how you and your husband, wife, boyfriend, or girlfriend are different from, or similar to, the people on pages 84–85.

Part 3 Practical English

Using Inclusive Language

UNDERSTANDING LANGUAGE AND SEXISM

Sexism is the belief that one sex, or gender (male or female), is better than the other sex. Language can express or add to sexism. Some common phrases in English traditionally name men first, for example, "men and women," "husbands and wives," and "Mr. and Mrs."

There are also words for jobs that refer only to men—words such as *fireman* and *postman*. These words do not include the idea of women fighting fires or delivering the mail. Therefore, most people now say *fire fighter* and *mail carrier* to include both men and women. To make language more equal, or *gender-neutral*, people are changing many words and the way that we use some language.

1 Matching Words Read the words below. Match the words in Column A with the gender-neutral words in Column B.

Column A (only male or only female)   **Column B** (either male or female)

1. __*f*__ man-made   **a.** chair or chairperson
2. _____ mankind   **b.** salesclerk
3. _____ policeman   **c.** spouse
4. _____ chairman   **d.** police officer
5. _____ actress   **e.** fisher
6. _____ wife or husband   **f.** synthetic, manufactured, machine-made
7. _____ housewife   **g.** server in a restaurant
8. _____ salesman   **h.** humanity, people, human beings
9. _____ waiter/waitress   **i.** actor
10. _____ fisherman   **j.** homemaker

USING GENDER-NEUTRAL POSSESSIVE ADJECTIVES

Possessive adjectives show gender: *his* is used for a male, *hers* is used for a female. But sometimes we don't know if the noun is a male or a female. In such cases, you can say *his or her*. Or you can make the noun plural and use the possessive adjective *their*, which can be male or female.

Examples

Every student should remember **his** book.

    (*His* refers to a male. We can use this only when every student is a male.)

Every student should remember **his or her** book.

    (Using *his or her* includes both male and female students.)

Students should remember **their** books.

    (Using the gender-neutral possessive adjective *their* includes both male and female students.

---

2 Using Possessive Adjectives Read the sentences below. Write *his*, *her*, or *his or her* in the blanks. Then rewrite sentences 1, 4, 7, and 9 by changing the subject, verb, and object if necessary and by using the pronoun *their*.

1. A smart student keeps _____*his or her*_____ papers in _____ notebook.

    _____*Smart students keep their papers in their notebooks.*_____

2. The tall man left _____ book on the table.

3. The woman was angry at _____ husband.

4. A doctor will pay a lot of money for _____ education.

_____

5. Some police officer parked _____ car on the street in front of my house.

6. My teacher, Ms. Smith, always wears _____ glasses in class.

7. Every teacher needs to know _____ subject well.

_____

8. Mr. Jones is my teacher and I love _____ class.

9. Every person can make _____ own decision.

_____

10. A man can change _____ mind, and a woman can change _____ mind, too.

Part 4 Vocabulary Practice

1 **Reviewing Vocabulary** Read each sentence below and write *true* or *false*. New words from this chapter are underlined.

1. A conversation between a husband and wife is a public event. ___ *false* ___

2. If two people are talking, it's a conversation. _____

3. Fire and water are similar in many ways. _____

4. An order is a polite way to ask someone to do something. _____

5. Animals that live in groups may have a hierarchy. _____

6. When you apologize, you say "thank you." _____

7. Spouse is a nonsexist way to talk about a husband or wife. _____

8. If I have ten dollars and Fred has ten dollars, we each have an <u>equal</u> amount of money. _____

9. To say that a woman can be a police officer is an example of <u>sexism</u>. _____

10. You can use the word <u>actor</u> to talk about men or women who act. _____

Now rewrite the false sentences to make them true.

Example

A conversation between a husband and wife is not a public event. (*or* A conversation between a husband and wife is a private event.)

 2 **Listening and Focusing on High-Frequency Words** Listen and fill in the blanks in the sentences. Some of the words are new and some of the words are not new. Then check your work on page 82.

Many people _____ that women talk more than
1
men do. _____ to Deborah Tannen, this isn't exactly
2
_____. She says women talk more than men only in
3
_____ situations—at home, with family, or with a few
4
friends. In _____ situations—in other words, in a big
5
group or at work, *men* talk more. Tannen says that men and
women often talk for _____ reasons. Men talk to give
6
or get information. They also _____ to get or keep a
7
high position among other men. But for women, people and
_____ are important. Women often talk to socialize
8
and _____ interest and love. They also talk to keep
9
their _____ relationships with friends and family.
10

3 **Completing Sentences** Read the words in the box and then read the sentences below. Write the correct word from the box in each of the blanks. Remember to read the whole sentence before you answer. These vocabulary words are from Chapters 1 through 5.

beverages	full time	married	scientists
cancer	garage	online	shopping
divorce	health	politics	uninteresting
families	lonely	quit	

1. Some ___scientists___ are doing important studies about _____, diabetes, and other diseases.

2. Many couples don't see each other very often because both people have to work _____. They may feel tired and _____ as a result.

3. Some _____—green and black tea, for example—have antioxidants and are good for your _____.

4. Traditional _____ are having trouble; _____ is going up, and fewer people are getting _____.

5. Jeff Bezos _____ his job and started Amazon.com in a _____.

6. Some people enjoy talking about world _____, but other people find that topic _____.

7. Many people are _____ for books and even cars _____ these days.

4 **Building Vocabulary** Complete the crossword puzzle. These words are from Chapters 1 through 5.

active	equal	marriage	sexism
big	good	phrase	similar
brag	hierarchy	position	socialize
conversation	high	private	suggestions
different	love	public	writer

Across

2. the opposite of *private*; when many people are around (adj.)

3. people talking (n.)

6. the opposite of *public*; when other people are not around (adj.)

7. a person who writes (n.)

10. having the same position (adj.)

14. meet with other people, talk, etc. (v.)

15. the belief that one sex is better than the other (n.)

17. opposite of *bad* (adj.)

18. legal agreement joining two people (n.)

Down

1. opposite of *hate* (v. and n.)

2. a group of words (n.)

4. a system in which there is higher or lower position (n.)

5. opposite of *same* (adj.)

8. ideas to make something better (n.)

9. say very good things about yourself (v.)

11. moving around a lot; doing many things (adj.)

12. opposite of *small* (adj.)

13. place in a social hierarchy (noun)

14. opposite of *different* (adj.)

16. opposite of *low* (adj.)

KEY: *adj.* = adjective; *adv.* = adverb; *n.* = noun; *prep.* = preposition; *v.* = verb

Self-Assessment Log

Read the lists below. Check (✓) the strategies and vocabulary that you know. Look through the chapter or ask your instructor about the other strategies and words.

Reading and Vocabulary-Building Strategies

- ❑ Understanding humor
- ❑ Understanding new words in a reading
- ❑ Identifying the main ideas and details
- ❑ Identifying a good summary
- ❑ Identifying details
- ❑ Reading faster
- ❑ Understanding language and sexism
- ❑ Using possessive adjectives

Target Vocabulary

Nouns	Verbs	Adjectives	Adverb
❑ conversations	❑ apologize	❑ active*	❑ full time
❑ feelings*	❑ brag	❑ close*	
❑ hierarchy	❑ socialize	❑ equal*	**Preposition**
❑ orders*		❑ lonely	❑ according to*
❑ politics*		❑ private*	
❑ position*		❑ public*	
❑ sexism		❑ similar	
❑ spouse		❑ uninteresting	
❑ suggestions*			

---

*These words are among the 1,000 most-frequently used words in English.

Sleep and Dreams

You will read about something that we all do—sleep. What happens when we sleep? Everyone does not agree on this answer. In Part 1 of this chapter, you will read about some theories and research on sleep and dreams. In Part 2, you will read a person's dream narrative. You will learn about doing a search on the web in Part 3. As in every chapter, you will get a chance to practice the vocabulary and do a crossword puzzle in Part 4.

❝ Dreams say what they mean, but they don't say it in daytime language. ❞

—Gail Godwin
American writer (1937–   )

Connecting to the Topic

1 What do you see in the photo? What are the people doing?

2 What are four questions that the researcher (the man in the white coat) might have about sleep and dreams? Discuss them.

3 What do you think happens when we sleep?

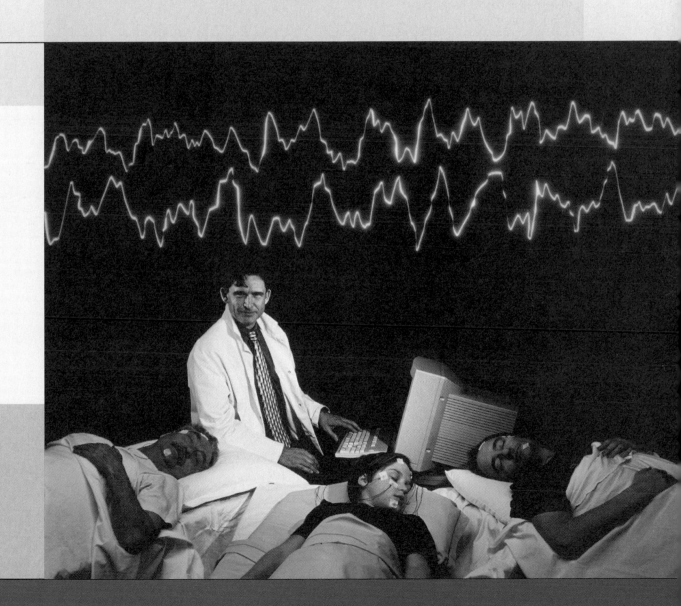

The Purpose of Sleep and Dreams

Before You Read

1 Interviewing Students Look at the questions in the chart below. Decide on your answers. Then walk around the room and ask four students the questions. Put their answers in this chart.

Questions	Student 1	Student 2	Student 3	Student 4
1. How many hours of sleep do you need each night?				
2. Why do we sleep?				
3. Does everyone dream?				
4. What do you think a road in a dream means?				

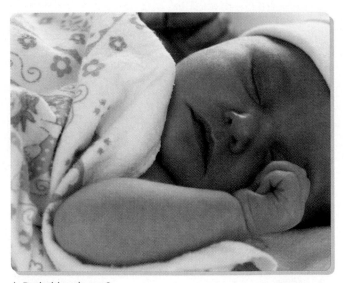

▲ Do babies dream?

2 Previewing Vocabulary Read the words in the list. They are words from the next reading. Listen to their pronunciation. Do not look them up in a dictionary. Check (✓) the words that you know.

Nouns		Adjective	Adverb
❑ childhood	❑ stage	❑ awake	❑ however
❑ desires	❑ symbols		
❑ emotions	❑ theories (theory)		
❑ evidence	❑ vision		
❑ Freud	**Verbs**		
❑ hormone	❑ occurs		
❑ logic	❑ predict		
❑ psychologists	❑ repair		
❑ purpose	❑ wonder		
❑ research			

3 Understanding New Words In Chapters 1–5, you learned ways to understand new words in a reading. Below are some new words from the next reading. Try to understand their meanings from these sentences, without a dictionary. Write the meanings on the lines.

1. Many people <u>wonder</u>: Why do we sleep? Why do we dream? They ask themselves about the reasons for sleep and dreams.

   wonder = *to question or ask yourself something*

2. There was a lot of <u>evidence</u> that George killed Mr. Smith. Police found George's gun in Mr. Smith's house. Also, two people saw George leaving Mr. Smith's house. In addition, everyone knew that George hated Mr. Smith.

   evidence = _____

3. Our bodies produce more of a growth <u>hormone</u> (a chemical that helps us grow) while we sleep.

   hormone = _____

4. Some people think that dreams are important; <u>however</u>, other people think that dreams have no meaning and aren't important.

   however = _____

5. A <u>psychologist</u> studies people's behavior. Some psychologists, such as Sigmund Freud, have strong beliefs about dreams.

   psychologist = _____

6. Can dreams tell us something about our <u>emotions</u>—our feelings?

   emotions = _____

7. Maybe these are <u>symbols</u>. In other words, they mean *other* things. For example, a road in a dream might be a symbol of the dreamer's life.

   symbols = _____

8. When we are <u>awake</u>, we don't dream. We dream only when we're asleep.

   awake = _____

9. Those parts of the brain are for <u>vision</u> (the ability to see), and <u>logic</u> (the ability to think and understand).

vision = _____

logic = _____

Strategy

Finding the Meaning of New Words: Meaning After *Or*
You do not always need to use a dictionary to find the meaning of a new word. The meaning of a new word is sometimes after the word *or*.

Example
> There are many **theories**, or opinions.
> (**Theories** means opinions.)

---

4 **Finding the Meaning of New Words** The meanings of these words are in the next article. Find the words and circle their meanings.

purpose	repair	occurs	stage	desires	research

Read

5 **Reading an Article** Read the following article. Don't use your dictionary. If you don't know some words, try to figure out their meanings. Then do the exercises.

The Purpose of Sleep and Dreams

A Many people **wonder**: Why do we sleep? Why do we dream? They ask themselves the **purpose**, or reason. There are many **theories**, or opinions, about this, but scientists don't know if these ideas are correct.

Theories of Sleep

B One theory of sleep says that during the day, we use many important chemicals in our bodies and brains. We need sleep to make new chemicals and **repair**, or fix, our bodies. This theory is called the "Repair Theory." One piece of **evidence** for this theory is that our bodies produce more of a growth **hormone** (a chemical that helps us grow) while we sleep. Another theory is that the purpose of sleep is to dream. Dreaming **occurs**, or happens, only during one **stage**, or period, of sleep—REM (Rapid Eye Movement) sleep. 10

5

REM sleep occurs about every 90 minutes and last for about 20 minutes. Some scientists believe that REM sleep helps us to remember things, but other scientists don't agree.

Dream Theories

C   Whatever the reason for sleep, everyone sleeps, and everyone dreams every night. Many times we don't remember our dreams, but we still 15 dream. Like sleep, no one knows exactly why we dream or what dreams mean. There have been many theories about dreams throughout history. Many cultures believe that dreams can **predict** the future—that they can

▲ Dreams occur only during REM sleep.

tell us what is going to happen to us. **However,** 20 some people believe that dreams are only a form of entertainment.

D   **Psychologists** such as Sigmund **Freud** say that 25 dreams are not predictions of the future. Psychologists have strong beliefs about dreams. However, these scientists don't always 30 agree with each other. There are several different theories about the purpose of dreaming.

E   Freud, who wrote around the year 1900, said that dreams can tell us 35 about our **emotions**—feelings—and **desires**, or wishes. Freud believed that our dreams are full of **symbols**. In other words, things in our dreams mean *other* things. For example, a road in a dream isn't really a road. It might be a symbol of the dreamer's life. Freud thought that dreams are about things from our past, from our **childhood**. Other psychologists say 40 no. They believe that dreams are about the *present*, about our ideas, desires, and problems *now*. Other psychologists say that dreams have no meaning at all.

New Evidence

F   We still don't know why we dream. However, there is interesting new evidence from **research**, or studies, about the brain. When we are **awake**, 45 many parts of our brain are active, for example the parts for emotions, **vision** (the ability to see), **logic** (the ability to think and understand), and others. However, when we are asleep and dreaming, the part of the brain for *logic* is not active. Maybe this new evidence answers one common question: Why do dreams seem so crazy? 50

After You Read

6 Finding Details What are some theories about sleep and dreams? Look back at the reading. Find information and fill in this chart.

Theories	
Why do we sleep?	1.
	2.
Why do we dream?	1.
	2.
	3. *Freud said:*
	4.
	5.

7 Working with New Words Write the vocabulary words for the meanings below. For help, look back at the boldfaced words in the reading. (Look before the word *or*.)

Meaning	Vocabulary Word
1. reason	
2. opinions	
3. fix	
4. happens	
5. period of time	
6. wishes	
7. studies	

Understanding Words from Their Parts

The beginning or ending of some words can help you with their meanings. Here are four:

Word Part and Meaning	Example
■ *un-* can mean "not"	**un**happy
■ *-er* can mean "a person who"	writ**er**
■ *-ist* can mean "a person who studies something or knows a lot about it"	scient**ist**
■ *-hood* can mean "the situation or stage of life when a person . . ."	parent**hood**

8 **Understanding Words from Their Parts** Write a word for each definition below. Use a word in the definition and a part from the Strategy Box above: *un-, -er, -ist, -hood*.

1. not interesting = *uninteresting* _____

2. a person who dreams = _____

3. the stage of life when a person is a child = _____

4. a person who knows a lot about psychology = _____

5. not comfortable = _____

6. a person who does research = _____

9 **Discussing the Reading** Talk about your answers to the following questions.

1. Do you remember your dreams? What do you think dreams mean?

2. What does your family or culture think about dreams?

3. Do you believe one of the theories from Activity 6 about why we dream? Why or why not?

A Dream Narrative

Before You Read

1 Thinking About the Topic For each question, choose the answer that is correct for you. Then share and discuss your answers with a group.

1. How often do you remember your dreams?
   - (A) every night
   - (B) often (four or five times a week)
   - (C) sometimes (once or twice a week)
   - (D) rarely (once a month)
   - (E) never

2. How often do you have nightmares (dreams that are scary or frightening)?
   - (A) every night
   - (B) often (four or five times a week)
   - (C) sometimes (once or twice a week)
   - (D) rarely (once a month)
   - (E) never

3. How often do you talk about your dreams with friends or relatives?
   - (A) every time I dream
   - (B) often
   - (C) sometimes
   - (D) rarely
   - (E) never

4. How often do you try to interpret your dreams—in other words, to figure out the meaning?
   - (A) every time I dream
   - (B) often
   - (C) sometimes
   - (D) rarely
   - (E) never

2 Previewing Vocabulary Read the words in the list. They are words from the next reading. Listen to their pronunciation. Do not look them up in a dictionary. Check (✓) the words that you know.

Verbs	Adjectives	Adverb	Idiom
❑ realized	❑ anxious	❑ outside	❑ make sense
❑ traveling	❑ complicated		
	❑ familiar		
	❑ unfamiliar		

Finding the Meaning of New Words in Context

Sometimes the meaning of a word can be found in the sentence or phrase that follows the new word.

Example

> We had our lunch **outside**. It was a warm day, and we sat under a tree.
>
> (*outside* = not on the inside of something; not in a building)

3 **Finding the Meaning of New Words in Context** Find the meaning of the underlined words. Look in the sentence or phrase that follows them. Choose the best answer.

1. My friends like to <u>travel</u>. Last week they went to Hong Kong. I prefer to stay here in my own city on my vacation.

   (A) study   (B) go places   (C) exercise

2. I was very <u>anxious</u>. This always happens to me. I'm always very worried before an exam.

   (A) happy   (B) busy   (C) nervous

3. I was in a new city. Everything was strange. Nothing was <u>familiar</u>.

   (A) from my family   (B) something that I knew   (C) beautiful

4. The math problem was very <u>complicated</u>. I couldn't do it, and my teacher couldn't do it, either.

   (A) easy   (B) interesting   (C) difficult

5. You can't stay home today! Don't you <u>realize</u> that we have a really important exam?

   (A) understand   (B) want   (C) wonder

6. The story didn't <u>make sense</u>. I read it four times, and I still didn't understand it.

   (A) easy to understand   (B) interesting   (C) without logic

Read

4 **Reading a Narrative** Read this narrative (story). Then answer the questions.

A Dream Narrative

▲ Writing a dream journal

A   This is the dream of a 40-year-old businessman. He is married and has two children. He goes to a psychologist because he feels **anxious** a lot. The psychologist told him to write down his dreams. This is his dream from June 7.   5

B   *Dream 6/7: In my dream I was in a large city. It was very big and very dark. The city seemed like New York, but it didn't look like the real New York. I was in a friend's apartment. It was comfortable. After a few minutes, I left and went out on the street, alone. I 10 walked for a while. Then I realized I was lost. I couldn't find my friend's apartment again. I started to feel uncomfortable. I tried to return to the apartment, but all of the streets looked unfamiliar and completely different, and I didn't know my friend's address. I began 15 to feel anxious.*

C   *I kept walking. I wanted to find something familiar. It was getting late. I decided to go home. I knew my home was outside the city. I saw buses on the street, but I didn't know which one to take. I couldn't find a way to leave the city. There was a way to get home, but I 20 didn't know it. I asked for directions. The people answered, but they didn't make any sense. All their directions were very complicated, and I couldn't understand them.*

D   *Suddenly I was on a boat. The boat was traveling across a very dangerous river. It was dark. The river was very dirty. There was garbage in it. I couldn't 25 see the other side of the river, and I was afraid. I began to think, "I'll never get home." I tried to ask for help, but no one listened to me. Then I woke up.*

After You Read

5 **Identifying the Main Idea** What is the main idea of the reading?

   Ⓐ A businessman was in a big city at night.
   Ⓑ A man wrote about his dream for his psychologist.
   Ⓒ A man was trying to go home, but it was difficult.

104   Chapter 6 ■ ■ ■

6 **Finding Details** Read the dream narrative again. Then read the details below. Put checks (✓) next to the details that are in the narrative.

_____✓_____ The man was anxious.

_____ A psychologist tried to help him.

_____ He walked to his psychologist's office in the city.

_____ In his dream, he was in a big city.

_____ It was morning in his dream.

_____ In the dream, he wanted to go home.

_____ In the dream, he had problems on his way home.

7 **Understanding Pronouns** Find the meaning of each underlined pronoun. Highlight it. Then draw an arrow from the pronoun to its meaning.

1. The city seemed like New York, but it didn't look like the real New York.

2. I was in a friend's apartment. It was comfortable.

3. On the street I saw buses, but I didn't know which one to take.

4. There was a way to get home, but I didn't know it.

5. All their directions were very complicated, and I couldn't understand them.

UNDERSTANDING MOOD

The *mood* of a piece of writing is the "feeling," or emotion in it. One way to understand the mood is to notice the adjectives. For example, a writer might use the adjectives *happy, wonderful*, and *beautiful* for a positive mood or *anxious, unhappy,* and *horrible* for a negative mood.

---

8 **Understanding Mood** Find all of the adjectives in the dream narrative. Highlight them. In your opinion, what is the mood of this dream?

9 **Discussing the Reading** Look back at Paragraph E on page 99. Then talk about your answers to the following questions.

1. What might psychologists say about the man's dream on page 104? What are his emotions?

2. What might be some symbols in his dream? In your opinion, what might they mean?

10 Writing in Your Journal Choose one topic below. Write about it for five minutes. Use some of the vocabulary that you have learned in this chapter.

- something that you learned about sleep or dreams
- a dream that you have had
- your opinion of dreams

Part 3   Practical English

Searching the Web

Using the Internet

Searching for Information on the Internet
Searching the Web is difficult, especially in a foreign language. Some websites are useful and some are not useful. When you do a search, look at the search results page. You need to scan the information—read very quickly and get a general idea of each website. Then decide if it is useful to you.

Example
Below is an example of a search results page on the Internet. Note the meaning of the following terms on the websites:

    .com = commercial (indicates a business)

    .org = organization (an organization, not usually a business)

    .edu = education (indicates a college or university)

SEARCH: dreams
Search results

1. Amazon.com: Akira Kurosawa's Dreams (1990): DVD
   Short films by the famous Japanese director . . . www.amazon.com

2. What Dreams Are Made Of - Newsweek Health - MSNBC.com
   Article on the study and history of dreams, Newsweek Magazine . . .
   www.msnbc.msn.com

3. Dreams Bed Superstore
   Dreams is Britain's leading bed seller, selling a wide range of beds. Sells all types and kinds of beds . . . www.dreamsplc.com

4. Dreams: FAQ

This site will answer most of your general questions about dreams. . . .
people who did that research in the 1950s and . . .
psych.ucsc.edu/dreams/FAQ International Conference

5. The DREAMS Foundation

(Dream Research and Experimental Approaches to the Mechanisms of Sleep)
This dream blog is pretty amazing . . . bloggers across the Internet have
written down their dreams. . . . dreams.blogharbor.org

6. Dreams and Wishes Quotes

Quotes and quotations from the website Famous Quotes . . . All our dreams
can come true, if we have the courage to pursue them. Walt Disney
www.goodquotes.com/~.htm

1 **Searching for Information on the Internet** You are in a college freshman
psychology course. You have to do a four-page research paper about dreams. Match
each website description below to a website in the Strategy Box on page 106 and 107.
Write the number of the site on the line.

a. __2__ This site has an article from a popular news magazine. It is probably a
good place for basic information about the subject.

b. _____ The Web address of this site has "ucsc.edu". The "edu" tells us it is
probably a university. It answers "frequently asked questions" (FAQ)
and so it is probably a good place for basic information.

c. _____ This website sells books and movies. This site is on the list only because
the title of the movie is "Dreams."

d. _____ On this website, people can describe their dreams and share them with
other people. It might be useful for our research.

e. _____ This is a site with quotes about different subjects. This page gives us
quotes about dreams. It would not be useful.

f. _____ This site sells beds. It is not at all useful.

What are the three best sites for your research paper? Write your choices below.

_____

_____

_____

2 Choosing Words for a Web Search Using more than one word in your search can help you find good sites. Look at the words in the box and circle or highlight the words you think would help in the search in Activity 1.

baseball	Freud	research	theories
dreams	humans	sleep	university
freshman	paper	student	wake

Imagine you are writing a paper about new theories on the reason why people sleep. Write four words you might use to search the Internet. Choose words from the box above or think of other words. Share your answers with classmates. What are the best four words?

_____   _____

_____   _____

Part 4   Vocabulary Practice

1 Reviewing Vocabulary Read each sentence below. Check (✓) *True* or *False*. Vocabulary words from this and previous chapters are underlined.

	True	**False**
1. <u>Emotions</u> and feelings are almost the same.	❑	❑
2. If you're <u>awake</u>, you're not asleep.	❑	❑
3. If you use <u>logic</u>, you make decisions with your emotions.	❑	❑
4. An <u>anxious</u> person is not usually nervous.	❑	❑
5. <u>Childhood</u> is one <u>stage</u> in human life.	❑	❑
6. Most movies and stories have a <u>narrative</u>.	❑	❑
7. If you understand the class, it doesn't <u>make sense</u>.	❑	❑
8. If you have a <u>theory</u>, you should have some <u>evidence</u> for that theory.	❑	❑

 2 Listening: Focusing on High-Frequency Words Listen and write the missing words in the blanks on the next page. If you don't know, then guess. Check your answers on page 99, Paragraph E.

Freud, who wrote around the year 1900, said that dreams can tell us about our emotions—feelings—and _____, or wishes. Freud _____ that our dreams are full of symbols. In other words, things in our dreams mean *other* things. For example, a road in a _____ isn't really a road. It might be a _____ of the dreamer's life. Freud _____ that dreams are about things from our past, from our _____. Other psychologists say no. They _____ that dreams are about the *present*, about our ideas, desires, and problems *now*. _____ psychologists say that dreams have no meaning at all.

3 **Using Your Vocabulary** Use these words from Chapter 6 to make your own sentences.

1. stage / dreaming / occurs

Dreaming occurs during the REM sleep stage.

2. purpose / sleep / scientists

_____

3. cultures / predict / dreams

_____

4. dreams / psychologists / research

_____

5. childhood / I / often

_____

4 **Building Vocabulary** Complete the crossword puzzle. These words are from Chapters 3, 5, and 6.

aunt	desires	purpose	theory
average	evidence	repair	traditional
awake	Freud	research	unfamiliar
branch	logic	similar	vision
childhood	predict	stage	wedding

Across

1. opposite of *familiar* (adj.)

5. an idea a scientist has about something (n.)

9. opposite of *different* (adj.)

10. see ahead into the future (v.)

11. the sister of my mother (n.)

12. wishes, wants (n.)

16. opposite of *asleep* (adj.)

17. a famous psychologist (n.)

18. the method you use when you think carefully (n.)

19. proof that something is true (n.)

Down

2. scientific study (n.)

3. life from birth to age 18 (n.)

4. the ability to see (n.)

6. like the past (adj.)

7. Childhood is the first _____ of life. (n.)

8. fix; make something good again (v.)

11. The _____ of 3 and 9 is 6. (n.)

13. the reason for an action or a thing (n.)

14. a ceremony when people get married (n.)

15. something a family and a tree have (n.)

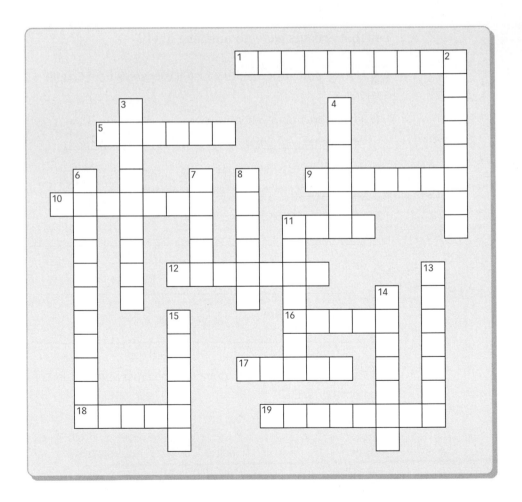

KEY: *adj.* = adjective; *adv.* = adverb; *n.* = noun; *prep.* = preposition; *v.* = verb

Self-Assessment Log

Read the lists below. Check (✓) the strategies and vocabulary that you know. Look through the chapter or ask your instructor about the other strategies and words.

Reading and Vocabulary-Building Strategies

❏ Finding the meaning of new words: meaning after *or*
❏ Finding details
❏ Understanding words from their parts
❏ Finding the meaning of new words in context
❏ Identifying the main idea
❏ Understanding pronouns
❏ Understanding mood
❏ Searching for information on the Internet

Target Words

Nouns
❏ childhood*
❏ desires*
❏ emotions
❏ evidence
❏ Freud
❏ hormone
❏ logic
❏ psychologists
❏ purpose*
❏ research
❏ stage*
❏ symbols
❏ theories (theory)
❏ vision

Verbs
❏ occurs
❏ predict
❏ realized*
❏ repair
❏ traveling (travel)*
❏ wonder*

Adjectives
❏ anxious
❏ awake
❏ complicated
❏ familiar*
❏ unfamiliar

Adverbs
❏ however
❏ outside*

Idiom
❏ make sense

*These words are among the 1,000 most-frequently used words in English.

Work and Lifestyles

In This Chapter

Have you ever volunteered your time? In this chapter, you will read about people who volunteer. They work and spend their time to help others, but they don't receive money. In Part 1, you will learn about different things that volunteers can do and who they can help. In Part 2, you will read about the personal experience of one young volunteer. In Part 3, you will have practice reading charts and comparing how much money countries have and how much people in those countries volunteer. Finally, Part 4 provides opportunities to work with new vocabulary.

❝ Success in life has nothing to do with what you gain in life or accomplish for yourself. It's what you do for others. ❞

—Danny Thomas
American entertainer (1914–1991)

Connecting to the Topic

1 Describe the photo. Name everything that you see.

2 Why does this man need free food and water? What do you think happened?

3 What other things can people do to help each other?

Volunteering

Before You Read

1 **Thinking About the Topic** Look at the photos and discuss the questions.

1. What are five things that you see in each photo?

2. Who are these people?

3. What are they doing? Why?

▲ "Let's plant it here."

▲ "Can I get you anything?"

▲ "Would you like some soup?"

2 **Previewing Vocabulary** Read the words in the list. They are words from the next reading. Listen to their pronunciation. Do not look them up in a dictionary. Check (✓) the words that you know.

Nouns
- ☐ AIDS
- ☐ environment
- ☐ hardships
- ☐ homelessness
- ☐ lives (life)
- ☐ mammals
- ☐ teenagers
- ☐ volunteers

Verbs
- ☐ delivering (deliver)
- ☐ planted (plant)
- ☐ prepare
- ☐ release
- ☐ volunteer

Adjectives
- ☐ famous
- ☐ homeless
- ☐ lonely

Adverb
- ☐ daily

Expression
- ☐ take care of

Strategy

Finding the Meaning of New Words: Looking at Colons

You do not always need to use a dictionary to find the meaning of a new word. Sometimes a colon (:) can help you to understand a new word. If you know the key word or words on *one* side of the colon, then you can figure out the meaning of the word or words on the *other* side of the colon.

Examples

There are terrible **afflictions**: AIDS, cancer, and TB.

    What are some examples of afflictions? *AIDS, cancer,* and *TB*

She cooked some wonderful foods: **stews**, **casseroles**, and **soufflés**.

    What are stews, casseroles, and soufflés? *some wonderful foods*

3 **Finding the Meaning of New Words** The meaning of these words is in the next article. Find the words and look before or after the colons for their meanings. Underline the meanings.

hardships	elm	eucalyptus	sea lions
pine	cypress	seals	sea otters

4 Reading an Article Read the following article. Don't use your dictionary. If you don't know some words, try to figure out their meanings. Then do the exercises.

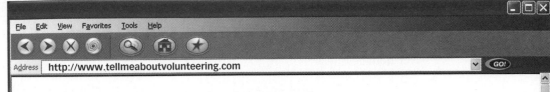

Address http://www.tellmeaboutvolunteering.com

Volunteering

A   Some people go to work each day and then come home. They spend time with their family and friends. Maybe they watch TV or go to a movie. Sometimes they exercise or read. This is their life. But for other people, this isn't enough. They look around their neighborhoods and see people with terrible **hardships**: sickness, loneliness, and **homelessness**. Other   5
people see problems with the environment. Many people want to help. They **volunteer**. They give some of their time to help others.

B   **Volunteers** help in many ways. Some visit sick and **lonely** people. Some give their friendship to children without parents. Some build houses for **homeless** people. Others sit and hold babies with **AIDS**.   10

C   Andy Lipkis was at summer camp when he **planted** his first tree. He began to think about the **environment**. In many countries, people were cutting down trees. Andy Lipkis worried about this. In 1974, he started a group, TreePeople, to plant trees: pine, elm, cypress, and eucalyptus. They also began to plant fruit trees in poor neighborhoods because fresh   15
fruit is often too expensive for poor people. Today there are thousands of members of TreePeople, and more join every day. They plant millions of trees everywhere to help the environment *and* people.

D   Ruth Brinker wasn't planning to change the world. Then a young friend became sick. He had AIDS. Soon he was very sick, and he couldn't   20
take care of himself. Brinker and other friends began to help him. In 1985, Brinker started Project Open Hand. This group cooks meals and takes them to people with AIDS. Soon Project Open Hand volunteers   25
were cooking many meals every day and **delivering** them to people who couldn't leave home. Today, volunteers **prepare** 2,000 meals **daily**. Ruth Brinker didn't plan to   30
change the world, but she is making a change in people's **lives**.

▲ Caring for a sick seal

E   Only three volunteers began the Marine Mammal Center in northern California in 1975. Today there are 800 volunteers. They work with **mammals**. Mammals are animals that feed on their mother's milk when young. The volunteers help sick ocean mammals: seals, sea lions, and sea otters. The sick animals become well and strong. Motherless baby animals grow big and healthy. For many weeks—or sometimes months—volunteers help to feed and take care of these animals. They also work in an educational program that teaches people about these animals. The volunteers don't get any pay for their hard work. Their "pay" is the good feeling on the day when they can **release** a healthy animal—take it to its home, the ocean, and let it go free.

F   Thirty or forty years ago, most volunteers were housewives. They volunteered time while their husbands were working. Today both men and women volunteer—and **teenagers** and children, too. There are volunteers from all social classes, all neighborhoods, and all ages. Most aren't rich or **famous**. They enjoy their volunteer work. People need them. Today, the world needs volunteers more than ever before. Perhaps a young Zulu boy from South Africa, Nkosi Johnson, said it best. Before he died of AIDS at the age of 12, he made a speech that is now famous. In this speech, he said, "Do all you can with what you have, in the time you have, in the place you are."

▲ Nkosi Johnson—small body, big heart

After You Read

5 **Identifying the Main Ideas and Important Details** Fill in this chart with information from the reading.

Name of the Organization	Who started it?	What do the volunteers do?	In which paragraph is this information?
TreePeople			

6 **Checking Vocabulary** Look back at the reading for the answers to these questions. (Look before or after the colons.)

1. What are three hardships? _____

2. What are pine, elm, cypress, and eucalyptus? _____

3. What are seals, sea lions, and sea otters? _____

Now write the word for the meanings below. For help, look back at the boldfaced words in the reading.

Paragraph	Meaning	Word
A	give time to help others	
C	the place around us	
D	taking things to people	
E	let an animal go free	
F	people between 13 and 19 years old	

SENTENCE STRUCTURE: UNDERSTANDING SENTENCES WITH THE WORD *THAT*

Sometimes a writer puts two sentences together with the word *that*.

Example

> They found a sick seal. + It was on the beach.
> They found a sick seal **that** was on the beach.

7 **Understanding Sentences with the Word *That*** Look back at Paragraph E to find a sentence with the word *that* for each pair of sentences below.

1. Mammals are animals. They feed on their mother's milk when young.

   _____

2. They also work in an educational program. It teaches people about these animals.

   _____

> **Culture Note**
>
> **Finding Places to Volunteer**
>
> Some people want to help others, but they wonder, How can I find a place to volunteer? In the United States, there is an organization called Volunteer Match. A person can go to their website, or other similar websites, and answer three questions:
>
> - What is your zip code (area of the country)?
> - How far can you travel to volunteer? (How many miles?)
> - What kind of volunteer work do you want to do? (Some possible answers are *animals*, *arts and culture*, *children*, *education*, *homeless people*, and *hunger*.)
>
> The website will give you a list of many organizations in your area.
> Are there websites like this in other countries that you know about?

8 **Discussing the Reading** Talk about your answers to the following questions.

1. Are any of the organizations in the reading interesting to you? If so, which one(s)? Why?

2. Do you (or does anyone you know) volunteer for any organization now, or did you in the past? Describe it.

Part 2 Reading Skills and Strategies

My Special Year

Before You Read

1 **Thinking About the Topic** Look at the photos on page 120. Answer the questions with another student.

1. These are photos of the same city. There are big contrasts—differences—between them. Describe the neighborhoods and the people. How are they different? Use adjectives.

2. All cities have good areas and bad areas. What are some contrasts in *your* city? Discuss two neighborhoods that are very different from each other. Use adjectives.

▲ What is life like for the people in these photos? ▲

2 **Previewing Vocabulary** Read the words in the list below. They are words from the next reading. Listen to their pronunciation. Do not look them up in a dictionary. Check (✓) the words that you know.

Nouns	**Verbs**	**Adjectives**
❏ contrast	❏ email	❏ fun
❏ crime	❏ taught (teach)	❏ tough
❏ drugs		
❏ energy		
❏ street children		

Read

3 **Reading a Narrative** Read this narrative. Then answer the questions.

My Special Year

A My name is Pablo. I think I'm a lucky guy. I have a good family, and we live in a nice neighborhood in a really special place, Puerto Vallarta, Mexico. People travel here from many countries for their vacations. We have beautiful beaches, hotels, restaurants, shopping, and sports.

B However, in my beautiful hometown, there are also very poor ⁵ neighborhoods. These areas are crowded and have a lot of crime. Life is terrible for many of the children in these areas. Some don't really have a childhood because they're homeless and live on the streets. They don't have families or education. They don't have enough food. Most of them have chronic stress. Many use drugs or have diseases or mental problems. ¹⁰

C Last year, I came back to Puerto Vallarta from my university in Mexico City. I spent one year as a volunteer with an organization called Outreach International. They have several programs. I volunteered for one program to help street children. It was the best—and most difficult—year of my life. I learned a lot that year. ¹⁵

D I worked in a home for street children (all boys, at this one). It's in an old school that nobody uses now. At this home, the boys have a place to sleep and three meals daily, but it's not a school. (They go to a neighborhood school.) The home keeps the boys off the streets. It shows them another way of life. As a volunteer, I helped to prepare meals. I taught games—such as basketball and ²⁰ football—and art. I helped the kids with their homework. These kids can be fun. They have a lot of energy, but they're also really tough. Their hardships on the streets make them strong and not always "sweet little children."

E At this boys' home, I met two other volunteers—Brian from Canada and Greg from Australia. In many ways, we were very similar. We were the ²⁵ same age, came from good homes, had a good education, and liked to travel. They were both college students, like me. We became friends. I helped them with Spanish, and they helped me with English. They came to meet my family, and we had fun together. Now, we email each other. But more than anything, I will always remember the children. I hope their lives ³⁰ can be better in the future. The contrast between their lives and my life is big. I hope they can have a good life, like I do.

After You Read

Strategy

Organizing Details Using a T-chart

In the reading, there were several contrasts and many details. You can use a T-chart to organize two sides of a topic.

Traveling

Good Things About It	Bad Things About It
fun	expensive
learn about new places	tiring
meet new people	miss home

4 Organizing Details Using a T-chart Complete the chart about Puerto Vallarta.

Puerto Vallarta

Good Things About It	Bad Things About It

5 Organizing Details Now make a T-chart to show the differences between the lives of the volunteers and the lives of the street children.

6 Thinking Critically: Making Inferences Read the sentences below. They are from the reading. Make guesses about street children from these sentences. Discuss your answers with a small group.

1. I worked in a home for these street children (all boys, at this one).

   What can you guess?
   - (A) The street children were happy at the home.
   - (B) Only boys live on the street.
   - (C) There is a different home for girls.
   - (D) I got money for my work.

2. These kids can be fun. They have a lot of energy, but they're also really *tough*. Their hardships on the streets make them strong and not always "sweet little children."

   What can you guess about the word *tough*? It means:
   - (A) fun and with a lot of energy
   - (B) strong
   - (C) sweet little children
   - (D) strong and not sweet

Strategy

Understanding Words from Their Parts: Suffixes
The ending of some words can help you with the meaning. These endings are called *suffixes*. Here are two: *-less* and *-ness*.

Word Ending and Meaning	Example
■ *-less* means "without"; words with *-less* are adjectives	home**less** (= with no home)
■ *-ness* means "a condition of"; words with *-ness* are nouns	homeless**ness** (= the condition of not having a home) happi**ness** (= the condition of being happy)

7 Understanding Words from Their Parts: Suffixes Write an adjective with the suffix *-less* on each line. Compare your answers with a partner.

1. The gum doesn't have sugar. It is _____*sugarless*_____.

2. He doesn't have a job. He is _____.

3. They don't have hope. They are _____.

4. He doesn't have a friend. He is _____.

5. She didn't get any sleep last night. It was a _____ night.

6. He doesn't have a heart. (He doesn't care about people.) He is _____.

7. The baby seal doesn't have a mother. She is _____.

8 Understanding Words from Their Parts: Suffixes Now write the correct words from the box on the following lines. Follow the example. (One word will not be used.)

home	homeless	homelessness
hope	hopeless	hopelessness
power	powerless	powerlessness

1. John lost his _____*home*_____. _____*Homelessness*_____ is a big problem in this city, and he felt very unhappy because he was _____.

2. When people become homeless they often lose _____ for the future. They begin to feel _____. _____ is a big problem for people living on the streets.

3. A sick person with no money often feels _____. This
_____ can cause depression and sadness.

9 **Discussing the Reading** Talk about your answers to the following questions.

1. What are some problems that street children (in any country) might have ?
Make a list.

2. In your opinion, is the situation hopeless? Why or why not?

3. What can we do to help poor people? List five things.

10 **Writing in Your Journal** Choose one topic below. Write about it for five
minutes. Use some of the vocabulary that you learned in this chapter.

- the problems of street children
- your ideas on how to help poor people
- one time when you were a volunteer
- one of the organizations from this chapter: TreePeople, Project Open Hand, The
Marine Mammal Center, Outreach International.

Part 3   Practical English

Reading Charts

1 **Reading a Chart** Read the information below and look at the chart about eleven
countries on page 125. Answer the questions that follow.

> The chart lists the percentage of people who volunteer in each country. It also
> lists information about the value of what each country produced in one year. This
> is called the Gross National Product (GNP.) The GNP per person is a country's
> yearly income divided by the population. See this example:
>   GNP = $5,000,000,000
>   Population: 50,000,000
>   GNP per person = $5,000,000,000 ÷ 50,000,000 = $100.00

Country	Percent of Population Volunteering	GNP Per Person
Brazil	12%	U.S. $4,630
Colombia	48	2,470
Finland	33	24,280
France	23	24,210
Germany	26	26,570
Israel	12	16,180
Japan	9	32,350
Netherlands	46	24,780
Sweden	51	25,580
Spain	12	14,100
U.S.	49	29,240

1. Which country has the highest percentage of volunteering?_____

2. Which country is the richest?_____

3. Which country is richer, Germany or Spain?_____

4. Which four countries have the lowest percentage of volunteering?

_____

5. Which country has a higher percentage of volunteers, Finland or Spain? _____

6. Which countries have four times the volunteers of Israel?_____

Discuss with a group what you notice about the answers. Is anything surprising?

2 **Working with Averages** The average GNP per person for the 11 countries on the chart is about $20,339. (The total amount of the GNP divided by the 11 countries.)

Germany is $6,231 above the average ($26,570 – $20,339 = $6,231), which is about 30 percent. Answer these questions about the chart.

1. How much above the average is Sweden? $_____
   (which is about 27% above)

2. How much below the average is Brazil? $_____
   (which is about 77% below)

3. What country is closest to the average? _____

4. Which country is most above the average? _____ How much? _____

5. Which country is the most below the average? _____ How much? _____

6. What is the average rate of volunteering among these eleven countries?_____

Part 4 Vocabulary Practice

1 Building Vocabulary The underlined words below are from this chapter. Circle the word in each group that does not belong or relate to the vocabulary word.

1. volunteer	work	(money)	help
2. tough	weak	strong	not nice
3. plant	cut down	grow	food
4. email	travel	computer	website
5. street children	lucky	poor	hungry
6. daily	weekly	early	monthly
7. young	child	childhood	sick
8. energy	power	weakness	strength
9. teach	educate	learn	show
10. drugs	coffee	pills	medicine
11. famous	unknown	popular	well known
12. fruit	lemon	carrot	banana
13. fun	enjoyable	boring	happy
14. lonely	cheerful	alone	by oneself

2 Listening and Focusing on High-Frequency Words Listen and fill in the missing words below. Then check your answers on page 116, paragraph D.

Ruth Brinker wasn't planning to _____ the world. Then a
                                        1

_____ friend became sick. He had AIDS. Soon he was very
        2

sick, and he couldn't _____ care of himself. Brinker and other
                            3

friends _____ to help him. In 1985, Brinker started Project
              4

Open Hand. This _____ cooks meals and takes them to people
                        5

with AIDS. Soon Project Open Hand volunteers were cooking many meals

every day and delivering them to people who couldn't leave home. Today,

volunteers _____ 2,000 meals _____. Ruth Brinker
                  6   7

didn't plan to change the _____, but she is making a change in
                                  8

people's _____.
              9

3 Filling in the Blanks Use the words in the box to complete the new paragraph about a kind man.

AIDS	hardships	homelessness	volunteering
crime	homeless	volunteer	volunteers

George works hard but he still finds time to _____ _____.
_1_
He _____ at a church in the middle of the city. There is a lot of
_2_
_____, like robbery and drug selling, so it is dangerous. There
_3_
is also a lot of _____, and people sleep on the street. The
_4_
_____ people have terrible _____. Some have diseases
_5_   _6_
like _____. George is _____ because he wants to
_7_   _8_
make a difference.

4 Building Vocabulary Complete the crossword puzzle with words from the box. These words are from Chapters 6 and 7.

AIDS	fruit	mammal	symbol
awake	hardships	plant	taught
contrast	homeless	release	tough
emotions	logic	research	vision
famous	lonely	rich	volunteer

Across

2. strong and able to take care of yourself (adj.)

4. examples: a human, a seal, or a dog (n.)

6. a big or strong difference (n.)

9. close, careful study of something (n.)

13. Scientists and mathematicians use this when they think. (n.)

14. with no home (adj.)

15. work for free (v.)

18. You do this to a tree or a seed. (v.)

19. Everybody knows about you; you are _____. (adj.)

20. examples: love, anxiety, joy (n.)

Down

1. a very serious disease (n.)

3. problems in life (n.)

5. When you're not sleeping, you're _____. (adj.)

7. the past tense of *teach* (v.)

8. examples: a lemon, an orange, a banana (n.)

10. examples: a flag or a red cross (n.)

11. the opposite of poor (adj.)

12. without any friends (adj.)

16. let something go (v.)

17. what you have because of your eyes (n.)

KEY: *adj.* = adjective; *adv.* = adverb; *n.* = noun; *prep.* = preposition; *v.* = verb

Self-Assessment Log

Read the lists below. Check (✓) the strategies and vocabulary that you know. Look through the chapter or ask your instructor about the other strategies and words.

Reading and Vocabulary-Building Strategies
- ❑ Finding the meaning of new words: looking at colons
- ❑ Identifying the main ideas and important details
- ❑ Understanding sentences with the word *that*
- ❑ Organizing details using a T-chart
- ❑ Making inferences
- ❑ Understanding words from their parts: suffixes
- ❑ Reading a chart

Target Vocabulary

Nouns
- ❑ AIDS
- ❑ contrast
- ❑ crime
- ❑ drugs
- ❑ energy
- ❑ environment
- ❑ hardships*
- ❑ homelessness
- ❑ lives (life)*
- ❑ mammals
- ❑ street children
- ❑ teenagers
- ❑ volunteers
- ❑ world

Verbs
- ❑ delivering
- ❑ email
- ❑ planted*
- ❑ prepare*
- ❑ release
- ❑ taught (teach)*
- ❑ volunteer

Adjectives
- ❑ famous*
- ❑ fun
- ❑ homeless*
- ❑ lonely
- ❑ tough

Adverb
- ❑ daily*

Expression
- ❑ take care of

* These words are among the 1,000 most-frequently used words in English.

8

Food and Nutrition

In This Chapter

You will read about something that we all need to do to stay alive. We all need to eat, but we don't all eat the same kinds of food. In Part 1, you will read about how people are changing their way of eating. In Part 2, you will read about some unusual things that people like to eat. You will have a chance to learn about what your classmates like to eat. In Part 3, you will read a chart about the calories and fat in some foods. Part 4 gives you a chance to work with new vocabulary.

❝ I've been on a diet for two weeks, and all I've lost is two weeks. **❞**

—Totie Fields
American comedian (1930–1978)

Connecting to the Topic

1 What are the people doing? What do you think they are saying?

2 What foods do you see in the photo?

3 What are four foods that you like to cook?

New Foods, New Diets

Before You Read

1 Interviewing Other Students Look at the questions in the chart below. Decide on your answers. Then walk around the room and ask four students the two questions. Write their answers in this chart.

Question	Student 1	Student 2	Student 3	Student 4
1. What foods do people eat now that people didn't eat 500 years ago?				
2. Are the foods that we eat now *more* or *less* healthful than 500 years ago?				

Strategy

Previewing a Reading
Before you read something, look it over quickly. Look at the pictures and read the titles and the headings (the titles for each paragraph or section.) This will give you ideas about the reading. With ideas in mind, you will understand more.

2 Previewing a Reading Read the questions below. Answer them with a partner by previewing the reading.

   1. What are the four headings?

   _____   _____

   _____   _____

   2. Look at the pictures. What are the people doing?

   3. What will the reading be about?

3 Previewing Vocabulary Read the words in the list. They are words from the next reading. Listen to their pronunciation. Do not look them up in a dictionary. Check (✓) the words that you know.

Nouns	Verbs	Adjectives	Conjunction
❑ centers	❑ gain	❑ attractive	❑ while
❑ diabetes	❑ join	❑ dairy	
❑ diet	❑ spend	❑ fried	
❑ irony		❑ raw	
❑ obesity		❑ slim	
❑ Rubens		❑ ugly	
❑ thousands			
❑ Titian			

Strategy

Using Opposites to Understand a New Word
Sometimes you can understand a new word if you know its opposite. If you know one of these words, you may not need a dictionary for the other.

Example
The people in the first picture aren't thin; they're **overweight**.
(The opposite of *thin* is *overweight*.)

4 **Using Opposites to Understand a New Word** Read the sentences. Then write the opposite of the underlined word.

1. People thought, How <u>attractive</u>!—not, How ugly!

    The opposite of *attractive* is _____.

2. Many of the vegetables are <u>raw</u>. They aren't cooked because cooking takes away some vitamins.

    The opposite of *raw* is _____.

3. People these days want to be <u>slim</u>, not fat.

    The opposite of *slim* is _____.

4. Sometimes people lose weight fast, but they usually <u>gain</u> it back again.

    The opposite of *gain* is _____.

Read

5 **Reading an Article** Read the following article. Don't use your dictionary. If you don't know some words, try to figure out their meanings. Then do the exercises.

New Foods, New Diets

Diet of the Past

A   On March 26, 1662, Samuel Pepys and four friends had lunch at his home in London, England. They ate beef, cheese, two kinds of fish, and six chickens. Today, we might wonder, "What? No fruits? No vegetables?" More than 300 years ago, people in Europe ate differently from today. They looked different, too. In famous paintings by **Titian**, **Rubens**, and other artists, people weren't thin; they were overweight. But people 300 years ago thought, "How **attractive**!"—not, "How **ugly**!" 5

▲ People in a 16th century painting

Today's Diet

B   Today, people are learning more about health. Many people are changing their ways of eating. They're eating 10 a lot of fruits and vegetables. Many of the vegetables are **raw**. They aren't cooked because cooking takes away some vitamins, such as vitamins A, B, and C. People are eating less sugar. They're eating low-fat foods. They're not eating much red meat. They're drinking less cola and coffee. 15

Trying to Be Thin

C   People these days want to be **slim**, not fat. Sometimes people in North America go a little crazy to lose pounds. **Thousands** of them **join** gyms and diet groups, go to special diet doctors, or **spend** a lot of money at diet **centers**. Each year Americans spend more than $46 billion on diets and diet products. 20

▲ People in a modern health club

More People Are Overweight

D   However, there is an **irony**—a surprising, opposite result—to all this dieting. **While** many people are becoming thin, other people are becoming overweight. *More* people are *overweight* than in the past! In many countries, there is a serious problem with **obesity**—in 25 other words, a condition of being very overweight. There are two main reasons. First, these days, many people often go to fast-food restaurants. (They didn't in the past.) At these restaurants, many of the foods (such as **fried** potatoes and meat) are high in fat. Some of the **dairy** products (such as cheese) are high in fat, and others (such as ice cream) 30 are high in fat *and* sugar. This seems similar to Samuel Pepys's party, doesn't it? Second, dieting doesn't often work. Sometimes people lose weight fast, but they usually **gain** it back again. Almost 95 percent of all people gain back weight after a diet. One problem with obesity is easy to see: overweight people have more sicknesses, such as heart disease and **diabetes**. 35

E   Sometimes people go crazy over food. Sometimes they eat very little because they want to be slim. Other times, they eat lots of bad foods because these foods taste good. When will people learn? Too much food, too little food, and the wrong foods are all bad ideas. 40

Culture Note

Vegetarians

Vegetarians are people who don't eat meat. Some vegetarians don't eat dairy products, either. In what countries or cultures is it easy to be a vegetarian? In what countries or cultures is it hard? If you are a vegetarian, why did you decide to be one? If you are not a vegetarian, would you consider becoming one?

After You Read

6 **Identifying the Topics** Read the topics below. Which paragraph is about each topic? Write the letter of the paragraph next to its topic.

1. _____ spending a lot of time and money on diets

2. _____ how people in Europe ate in the past

3. _____ conclusion

4. _____ a serious problem with weight in some countries

5. _____ foods for good health

7 **Working with New Words** Write the vocabulary words for the meanings below. For help, look back at the boldfaced words in the reading.

Paragraph	Meaning	Vocabulary Word
A	two famous painters	
D	a surprising, opposite result	
D	at the same time	
D	a condition of being very overweight	
D	a word for products from milk	
D	a sickness	

Organizing Details

When you organize notes and show the relationship of details, you can use graphic organizers like this one.

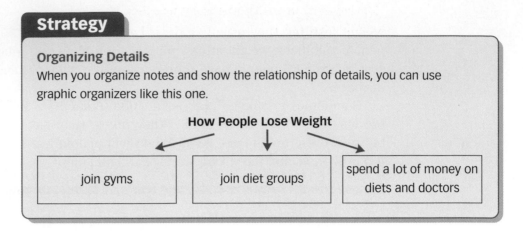

How People Lose Weight

| join gyms | join diet groups | spend a lot of money on diets and doctors |

8 **Finding Reasons** Look back at Paragraph D. Why are many people overweight these days? Find two reasons. Write them in the boxes below.

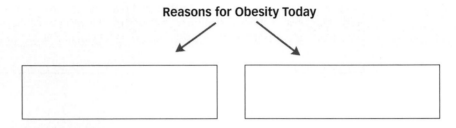

Reasons for Obesity Today

Figuring Out Words with More Than One Meaning

Many words in English have two or more meanings. Use the context to understand which meaning is correct in the sentence or paragraph where it is used.

Examples

I shouldn't eat all of this food. I'm on a **diet**.

　(Here, *diet* means eating less food than usual.)

A sea lion's **diet** is mostly fish.

　(Here, *diet* means the food that a person or animal usually eats.)

9 **Figuring Out Words with More Than One Meaning** What does the verb *work* mean in each sentence? Choose an answer for each sentence.

1. I have to <u>work</u> hard to stay thin.

　Ⓐ have a job

　Ⓑ be active and try

　Ⓒ succeed

2. Dieting often doesn't <u>work</u>. People usually gain back the weight.

　Ⓐ have a job

　Ⓑ be active and try

　Ⓒ succeed

3. They <u>work</u> in the entertainment business.

    (A) have a job

    (B) be active and try

    (C) succeed

10 Discussing the Reading Fill in the chart below about a culture that you know well. Then talk about it with a partner.

Meal	What do people usually eat and drink?	Are these different from foods in the past?
Breakfast		
Lunch		
Dinner		

Part 2   Reading Skills and Strategies

Eating Bugs

Before You Read

1 Previewing the Reading Look at the photos in the reading. What will the reading probably be about?

2 Interviewing Other Students Look at the questions in the chart below. Decide on your answers. Then walk around the room and ask three students. Write their answers in this chart.

Questions	Student 1	Student 2	Student 3
1. What are two of your favorite foods?			
2. Imagine that you can eat only one food for the rest of your life. What is it?			
3. What food do you dislike?			
4. What is one expensive, gourmet food that you like?			

3 **Previewing Vocabulary** Look at the words in the list. They are words from the next reading. Listen to their pronunciation. Do not look them up in a dictionary. Check (✓) the words that you know.

Nouns
❏ Asians
❏ bugs
❏ entomologists
❏ insects
❏ protein
❏ snacks

Verbs
❏ bake
❏ boil
❏ disgusts
❏ fry
❏ marinate

Adjectives
❏ delicious
❏ disgusting

Adverb
❏ worldwide

Conjunction
❏ except

Read

4 **Reading an Article** Read this article about bugs. Then complete the *After You Read* activities that follow.

Eating Bugs

A   Different cultures enjoy different foods. Sometimes a food that one culture thinks is **delicious** might seem **disgusting** to another. In much of the

▲ grasshopper

▲ caterpillar

▲ An ant

world, people eat beef, but the idea of meat from a cow **disgusts** some Hindus in India. People in France sometimes eat horsemeat or frogs, and this disgusts some Americans. People in Western countries eat cheese, and many 5 **Asians** think that this is disgusting. And then there are **insects**. Many people wonder, "How can people eat ***bugs***?" (Children in the U.S. make horrible faces and say, "Ooooh! Yucky!") However, insects are an important part of the diets in many countries.

B   In different places, people eat over 1,000 types of insects—and ate them 10 in the past, too. For example, people in ancient Greece and Rome ate insects. American Indians ate grasshoppers, crickets, and caterpillars. Today, in parts of Africa, people eat termites (insects that eat wood) and caterpillars as **snacks**. In Japan, some people eat grasshoppers with soy sauce. In small villages and in some restaurants in Thailand, people enjoy crickets and 15 grasshoppers. In some Mexican restaurants, people pay $25 for a plate of butterfly larvae. In the United States, some restaurants now offer insects as a gourmet food. In China, people spend $100 million each year on ants.

▲ Candy with insects

C   There are different ways to prepare bugs as food. One way is to **boil** them in very hot water. In 20 Colombia, some people spread them on bread. In the Philippines, people **fry** them in butter with vegetables. In Mexico, people fry them in oil or **marinate** them in lemon juice, salt, and chile. In some parts of Africa, some people **bake** or fry them. In other areas, they eat 25 them raw. (However, **entomologists**—scientists who study insects—say that it's important to cook insects, not eat them raw.) In the United States, a company called Hotlix now sells *candy* with insects in it.

D   Julieta Ramos-Elorduy, a researcher at a university 30 in Mexico City, says that there are many good reasons to eat **bugs**. First, insects are a cheap food (**except** on a plate in an expensive restaurant), and they taste good. Some insects taste like nuts, bacon, mint or cinnamon. Second, bugs are good for our health. For example, they often have more **protein** than beef or fish. Third, they can 35 bring money to poor people, who find them in the forest and sell them. In parts of Africa, there are seven pounds of insects on just one tree. This brings a good profit for very little work. Finally, eating insects can help to save the environment. In many countries, people cut down trees. However, they will not do this if the trees have insects to eat or sell. 40

E   People **worldwide** are now eating foods from other countries. People in the West now enjoy Japanese sushi (a small roll of cooked white rice served with a garnish of raw fish, vegetables, or egg). People everywhere eat Italian pizza and American hamburgers. Maybe someday, in a fast-food restaurant in any country, a customer will say, "Give me a hamburger and 45 an order of caterpillars, please." In the future, insects might be as familiar to us as rice, bread, or beans.

After You Read

Strategy

Finding the Main Ideas in a Reading
The main idea of a whole reading is usually in the first paragraph—the introduction. After that, each paragraph has a main idea, too, often in its first sentence. The last paragraph is the conclusion. It usually has one sentence that "finishes" the reading and might suggest a new idea, too.

5 Identifying the Main Ideas Read the main ideas below. Look back at the reading for the paragraph that expresses each of the main ideas. Then write the letter of the paragraph next to the main idea. Which of these ideas is the main idea of the whole reading? Put a check in front of that sentence.

1. _____ There are many reasons to eat insects.

2. _____ People in many countries eat insects.

3. _____ Foods such as insects are delicious to some people and not to others.

4. _____ In the future, people might eat insects everywhere, and they won't think it's strange.

5. _____ People prepare and eat insects in different ways.

6 Finding Details: Reasons Look back at Paragraph D. What are four reasons to eat insects? Write them in the boxes.

7 Finding Details Look back at the reading to find the answers to these questions.

1. In Paragraph C, how many ways can you find to prepare insects to eat? Write the ways on a piece of paper.

2. In the whole reading, how many types of insects can you find? Write their names on a piece of paper.

8 Checking Vocabulary Fill in the blanks with words from the box.

bugs	entomologists	protein
disgusting	except	worldwide

1. In the past, only the Japanese ate sushi. Now, people _____ eat it.

2. My little boy didn't want to eat the meat because he thought it was

   _____ , but we told him it was really very good.

3. Meat, fish, and insects have a lot of _____ , and this is necessary for good health.

4. _____ for Hindus, people in most cultures eat some amount of beef.

5. _____ study caterpillars, grasshoppers, ants, and other _____.

9 **Discussing the Reading** Talk about your answers to the following questions.

1. Is there some food from your culture that you think is disgusting? If so, what is it?

2. Do you eat anything that other people think is strange?

3. What is the strangest food that you have ever eaten?

10 **Writing in Your Journal** Choose one topic below. Write about it for five minutes. Use some of the vocabulary that you learned in this chapter.

- something that you learned about food
- your opinion of diets
- your opinion of eating insects
- the strangest thing that you have ever eaten

Part 3 Practical English

Reading Charts

1 **Reading a Food Chart** Look at the following chart. It lists the fat and calories in eleven types of food.

1. Which food has the most calories? _____

2. Which food has the least calories? _____

3. Circle the foods that you like.

Food Item	Calories	Fat (in grams)
apple (1)	80	.0
beef steak (3 oz.)	242	14.7
broccoli (3 1/2 oz.)	25	.2
chicken (baked leg)	130	4.7
chocolate chip cookie (1)	48	2
French fries (one serving)	200	10.0
grapes (1 bunch)	51	.1
milk (1 glass)	149	8.1
popcorn (2 cups, with butter)	85	12
potato chips (11)	140	11.0
tomato juice (small glass)	41	.1

2 Reading a Chart Look at the two pictures below and answer the questions about Bill and Maria. Use the food chart on page 141.

▲ Bill is eating dinner.

▲ Maria is eating dinner.

1. How many calories does Bill's steak have?   _____

2. How much fat does it have? (How many grams of fat?) _____

3. How many calories do Bill's French fries have? _____

4. How much fat do they have? (How many grams?) _____

5. How many calories does Bill's complete meal have? _____

6. How much fat does it have? (How many grams?) _____

7. How many calories does Maria's chicken have? _____

8. How much fat does it have? (How many grams of fat?) _____

9. How many calories do Maria's grapes have? _____

10. How much fat do they have? (How many grams)? _____

11. How many calories does Maria's complete dinner have? _____

12. How much fat does it have? (How many grams?) _____

13. You want to lose weight. Should you eat Maria's dinner or Bill's dinner?

_____

14. You want to eat less fat. Should you eat Bill's dinner or Maria's dinner?

_____

15. Bill's doctor wants Bill to eat about 500 calories for dinner. Create a dinner for Bill that is about 500 calories. What does it include?

_____

1 **Building Vocabulary** Read the words below. Circle the word in each line that does not belong in that group.

1. diabetes	heart disease	sickness	(health)
2. bugs	birds	insects	ants
3. overweight	slim	heavy	fat
4. boil	lose	bake	fry
5. protein	fat	sushi	calories
6. entomologist	scientist	protein	insect
7. worldwide	unattractive	not pretty	ugly
8. gain	add	lose	grow

2 **Listening and Filling in the Missing Words** Listen and fill in the words from the reading on page 134. Some of the words are new and some of the words are not new. Then check your answers.

However, there is an irony—a surprising, _____ result
 _1_
—to all this dieting. While many people are _____ thin,
 _2_
other people are becoming overweight. _____ people are
 _3_
overweight than in the past! In many countries, there is a _____
 _4_
problem with obesity—in other words, a _____ of being
 _5_
very overweight. There are two main _____. First, these
 _6_
days, _____ people often go to fast-food restaurants.
 _7_
(They didn't in the _____.) At these restaurants, many of
 _8_
the foods (_____ as fried potatoes and meat) are
 _9_
_____ in fat. Some of the dairy _____
 _10_   _11_
(such as cheese) are high in fat, and _____ (such as ice
 _12_
cream) are high in fat *and* _____. This seems similar to
 _13_
Samuel Pepys's party, _____ it? Second, dieting doesn't
 _14_
often work. Sometimes people _____ weight fast, but
 _15_

they usually _____ it back again. Almost 95 percent of all
                   16
people _____ back weight after a _____.
              17   18
One problem with _____ is easy to see: overweight people have
                        19
more _____ such as heart disease and diabetes.
            20

3 **Reviewing Vocabulary** Read each sentence and write *true* or *false*.

   1. Termites are <u>insects</u> that eat wood. _____

   2. Sushi usually has <u>fried</u> fish. _____

   3. If you <u>fry</u> something, you usually put it in oil. _____

   4. If you <u>gain</u> weight, you will weigh less. _____

   5. Vegetables usually have a lot of <u>calories</u>. _____

   6. People often eat chicken <u>raw</u>. _____

   7. If you <u>boil</u> something, you cook it in water. _____

   8. Ice cream is a <u>dairy</u> product. _____

▲ Does eating insects sound yummy or disgusting to you?

4 **Focusing on High-Frequency Words** Read the paragraph below and fill in each blank with a word from the box. When you finish, check your answers on page 134.

centers	join	people	spend
diet	lose	sometimes	thousands

_____ these days want to be slim, not fat. _____
 1   2

people in North America go a little crazy to _____ pounds.
                                                                        3

_____ of them _____ gyms and diet
               4   5

groups, go to special _____ doctors, or spend a lot of
                                  6

money at diet _____. Each year Americans
                       7

_____ more than $46 billion on diets and diet products.
       8

5 **Building Vocabulary** Complete the crossword puzzle on page 146 with words from the box. These words are from Chapters 7 and 8.

Asians	delicious	irony	slim
attractive	disgusting	motherless	snack
boil	environment	obesity	teenager
bugs	healthy	protein	ugly
cows	insects	raw	volunteer

Across

1. very hot water can do this (v.)

7. example: ants and crickets (n.)

10. the opposite of sick (adj.)

12. food that is uncooked (adj.)

13. condition of being very overweight (n.)

14. example: Chinese, Japanese, Koreans, Thai people (n.)

15. meat and fish have a lot of this (n.)

19. When you're 13 to 19 years old, you are a _____. (n.)

20. Old, rotten, and smelly food is _____. (adj.)

Down

2. when a surprising and opposite thing happens (n.)

3. Hindus don't eat these. (n.)

4. to do work without pay (v.)

5. tasting very, very good (adj.)

6. opposite of beautiful (adj.)

8. the air, trees, ocean—everything around us (n.)

9. nice to look at (adj.)

11. without a mother (adj.)

16. a little bit to eat, often between meals (noun)

17. thin or not fat (adj.)

18. insects (noun)

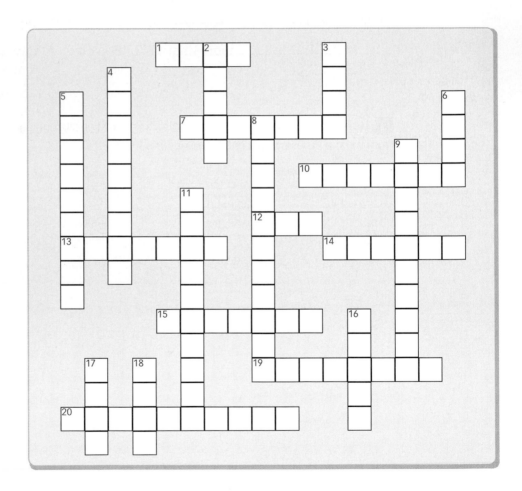

KEY: *adj.* = adjective; *adv.* = adverb; *n.* = noun; *prep.* = preposition; *v.* = verb

Self-Assessment Log

Read the lists below. Check (✓) the strategies and vocabulary that you know. Look through the chapter or ask your instructor about the other strategies and words.

Reading and Vocabulary-Building Strategies

❑ Previewing a reading
❑ Using opposites to understand a new word
❑ Identifying the topics
❑ Figuring out words with more than one meaning
❑ Organizing details using a graphic organizer
❑ Identifying the main ideas in a reading
❑ Finding details: reasons
❑ Reading a chart

Target Vocabulary

Nouns
❑ bugs
❑ calories (calorie)
❑ centers*
❑ diabetes
❑ doctors*
❑ entomologists
❑ insects
❑ irony
❑ obesity
❑ people*

❑ protein
❑ snacks
❑ thousands*

Verbs
❑ bake
❑ boil
❑ fry
❑ gain*
❑ join*
❑ lose*

❑ marinate
❑ spend*

Adjectives
❑ attractive
❑ dairy
❑ delicious
❑ disgusting
❑ fried
❑ raw
❑ slim

❑ ugly

Adverb
❑ worldwide

Conjunctions
❑ except*
❑ while

*These words are among the 1,000 most-frequently used words in English.

Great Destinations

In This Chapter

Get ready to think about vacations! In this chapter, you will read about exciting and adventurous vacations. Some people like to go to the beach or the mountains on their vacation. Others like to vacation in a city. What kind of vacation do you like? You will complete a personality questionnaire to find out what kind of vacation is perfect for you. You will also plan a dream vacation with classmates and read about and compare unusual vacation tours. You will also practice new vocabulary and do a crossword puzzle.

❝ Life is either a daring adventure or nothing. **❞**

—Helen Keller
American writer (1880–1968)

Connecting to the Topic

1 What country might they be in? What kind of vacation are they taking?

2 What are they looking at? What are they saying to each other?

3 What kind of vacation do you enjoy?

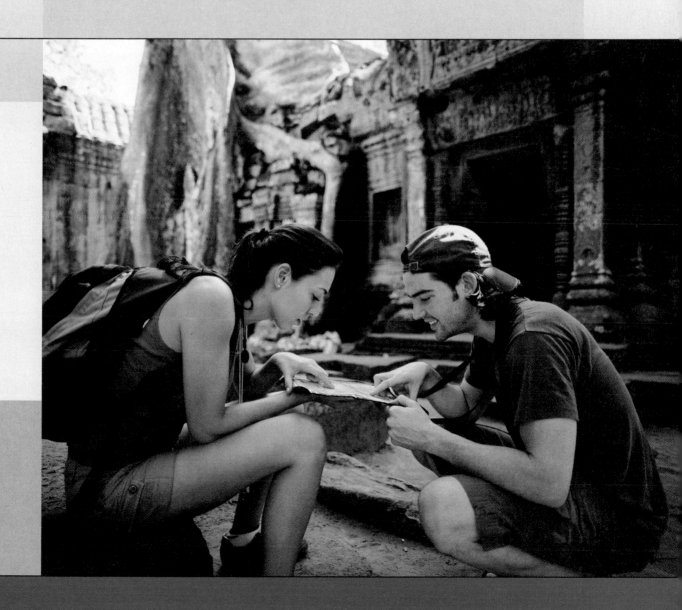

Adventure Vacations

Before You Read

1 Thinking About the Topic First, look over the pictures. Then, with a small group, answer the questions below.

1. Where are these people on vacation? What are they doing?

2. Which of these activities do you enjoy?

3. What do people like to do on vacation? Read the list of examples on page 151. Write two more things. Then circle all of the things that *you* like to do on vacation.

▲ Camping

▲ Sightseeing

▲ Shopping

▲ Hiking

stay at a nice hotel	go to movies or the theater
camp	meet new people
sightsee	learn new things
shop	_____
	_____

2 **Previewing the Reading** Look over the pictures and headings in the reading on pages 153–155. What kind of travel might this reading be about?

3 **Previewing Vocabulary** Read the words in the list. They are words from the next reading. Listen to their pronunciation. Do not look them up in a dictionary. Check (✓) the words that you know.

Nouns

- ❏ adventure
- ❏ amount
- ❏ archaeologists
- ❏ behavior
- ❏ biologists
- ❏ climate
- ❏ coast
- ❏ dolphins
- ❏ evidence

- ❏ glaciers
- ❏ ocean
- ❏ plants
- ❏ pollution
- ❏ prehistory
- ❏ seeds
- ❏ sightseeing
- ❏ species
- ❏ weather

Verbs

- ❏ count
- ❏ disappearing
- ❏ go camping
- ❏ go sightseeing
- ❏ prefer

Adjectives

- ❏ bored
- ❏ intelligent
- ❏ tropical
- ❏ worried

Adverb

- ❏ together

4 **Working with New Words** Figure out the meaning of each underlined word from the context. Choose the best answer.

1. I don't like the climate in that part of the country. It's too hot in the summer and too cold in the winter.
   climate:
   - (A) cities
   - (B) summer activities
   - (C) weather conditions

2. My neighbors' children have very good behavior. They're active, but they don't make a lot of noise, and they're always polite.
   behavior:
   - (A) way of acting
   - (B) health
   - (C) school work

3. Many things cause <u>pollution</u>—for example, factory smoke in the air and garbage in the water.

pollution:

- (A) rain and bad weather
- (B) new business
- (C) unhealthful things in the environment

4. There are twenty <u>species</u> of mammals, thirty-seven species of insects, and fifty-two species of plants in that area.

species:

- (A) kinds of animals
- (B) kinds of plants
- (C) kinds of living things

5. My wife likes the desert. My children like rivers and lakes in the mountains. But I <u>prefer</u> the <u>coast</u>, especially in summer, when I can go swimming.

prefer:

- (A) like
- (B) swim
- (C) dislike

coast:

- (A) cities
- (B) ocean beaches
- (C) forests

6. <u>Tropical</u> places such as Hawaii and Malaysia are beautiful and full of color, but they can be very hot, too.

tropical:

- (A) states in the United States
- (B) islands in the ocean
- (C) areas near the Equator (the circle around the earth that separates north from south)

UNDERSTANDING WORDS FOR DIRECTION

We use direction words to show the relationship of one area to another. If you know the words for the four basic directions, you can figure out four *other* directions. They are combinations of the basic four. See page 15 for the four basic directions.

---

5 **Understanding New Words for Direction** Use the information in the box above to answer these questions about four *other* directions.

1. What is a word for the direction between south and west? <u>southwest</u>

2. What is a word for the direction between south and east? _____

3. What is a word for the direction between north and west? _____

4. What is a word for the direction between north and east? _____

6 **Reading an Article** Read the following article. Don't use your dictionary. If you don't know some words, try to figure out their meanings. Then do the exercises.

Adventure Vacations

A   **P**eople like different kinds of vacations. Some **go camping**. They swim, fish, cook over a fire, and sleep outside. Others like to stay at a hotel in an exciting city. They go shopping all day and go dancing all night. Or maybe they **go sightseeing** to places such as Disneyland in the United States, the Taj Mahal in India, or the Louvre in France.   5

A Different Kind of Vacation

B   Some people are **bored** with sightseeing trips. They don't want to be "tourists." They **prefer** an **adventure**—a surprising and exciting trip. They want to learn something and maybe help people, too. How can they do this? Some travel companies and environmental groups are planning special adventures. Sometimes these trips are difficult, but they're a lot of fun. One   10 organization, Earthwatch, sends small groups of volunteers to different parts of the world. Some volunteers spend two weeks and study the environment. Others learn about people of the past. Others work with animals or **plants**.   15

▲ Collecting information

Hard Work in the Far North

C   Would you like an adventure in the Far North? Scientists are **worried** about changes in the **climate** worldwide. They are studying how the environment is changing because of a warming climate.   20 Two teams of volunteers (one in Alaska and the other in Iceland) will study **glaciers**— huge fields of ice that move very slowly. These glaciers are getting smaller. Scientists wonder why and how. Another   25 team will go to Manitoba, Canada. This

▲ Dolphins are intelligent ocean mammals.

▲ Archaeologists dig up an area for evidence of the past.

team will collect information on birds, mammals, and the **amount** of snow. If you like exercise and cold **weather**, these are good trips for you, but you must be in very good physical condition. 30

Studying Ocean Mammals

D Do you enjoy **ocean** animals? You can spend two weeks in Florida. There, you can study **dolphins**. It will be exciting to learn about these **intelligent** ocean mammals. These beautiful animals can live to over 50 years of age. They 35 travel **together** in family groups. From small boats, volunteers will study and photograph these groups. The purpose of this research is to learn about the animals' social **behavior**. Scientists want to know what dolphins do 40 and how they live. Also, scientists want to study dolphins' health. For example, they wonder, "Is ocean **pollution** changing the dolphins' health?" If you like warm weather, the ocean, and animals, this is a 45 good trip for you.

Digging Up the Past

E Are you interested in history or **prehistory?** Then southwest France is the place for your adventure. Between 35,000 and 250,000 years ago, early humans lived in 50 this area. Volunteers will work with **archaeologists** from France, Germany, and the United States to search for evidence about the way of life of the people from that time. If you choose this adventure, you will 55 dig for stone tools and bones, clean them, and photograph them. In your free time, you can travel around the beautiful countryside in the south of France.

Beaches and Biology

F Do you enjoy the beach and like to 60 learn about plants? There is an Earthwatch adventure in Yucatan, Mexico. On the north

coast of Yucatan, there are beautiful **species** of plants. Unfortunately, many of them are **disappearing**. People dig them up and sell them for large amounts of money. Mexican **biologists** need volunteers to collect **seeds**, **count** plants, and help to save several plant species. In your free time, you can travel to archaeological sites in the area. If you love a **tropical** climate, this is the trip for you. 65 70

G   Do you want a very different vacation? Do you want to travel far, work hard, and learn a lot? Then an Earthwatch vacation is for you. 75

▲ Biologists try to save plant species in Mexico.

After You Read

7 **Finding the Main Idea** Read the sentences below. Choose the main idea of "Adventure Vacations."

- (A) A trip with Earthwatch is a good way to learn something and have a vacation, too.
- (B) It's more fun to stay at a hotel than to go camping.
- (C) Disneyland, the Taj Mahal, and the Louvre are wonderful places to see on a vacation.
- (D) Earthwatch trips are difficult.

8 **Finding Details** Following are the main ideas of Paragraphs A, B, C, and D. Read the details below each main idea. Check (✓) all the details that are in each paragraph.

A: People like different kinds of vacations.

_____ Some people go camping.

_____ Some people swim, fish, cook over a fire, and sleep outside.

_____ Some people stay at a hotel in a city.

_____ Some people learn about neighborhood problems.

_____ Some people go shopping and dancing.

_____ Some people go to special places such as Disneyland.

B: Some people want an adventure.

_____ They want to stay at a hotel and go shopping.

_____ They want to learn something and maybe help people, too.

_____ Some groups plan special adventures.

_____ Earthwatch sends volunteers to different places in the world.

_____ Earthwatch volunteers help in shelters for the homeless.

_____ Earthwatch volunteers study the environment, work with animals, and learn about people of the past.

C: Teams of volunteers will study changes to the environment in the Far North.

_____ Two teams will study glaciers.

_____ The research will occur in Alaska, Canada, and Iceland.

_____ One team will study animals and snow.

_____ They will study rivers and lakes.

_____ Volunteers will need to be active in cold weather.

D: You can study dolphins in Florida.

_____ Dolphins are a species of fish.

_____ Dolphins live in family groups.

_____ Dolphins are intelligent.

_____ Scientists want to know more about the way that dolphins act with each other.

_____ Scientists want to know more about dolphins' health.

_____ Pollution is making dolphins sick.

9 **Working with New Words** Write the vocabulary words for the meanings below. For help, look back at the boldfaced words in the reading.

Paragraph	Meaning	Vocabulary Word
B	a surprising and exciting trip	
C	fields of ice that move very slowly	
C	how much of something there is	
D	a huge body of water	
F	going away	

Understanding Words from Their Prefixes

Some parts of words can help you to understand the meaning. Here are three: *pre-*, *archae-*, and *bio-*.

Prefix and Meaning	Example
■ *pre-* means "before"	**pre**view = to look at before
■ *archae-* means "very old, from the past"	**archae**ology = the study of things from the past
■ *bio-* means "life"	**bio**logy = the science of living things

10 **Understanding Words from Their Prefixes** Fill in the chart with three words from the reading.

Prefix	Word	Meaning
1. pre-		= a time before writing
2. archae-		= a scientist who studies very old times
3. bio-		= scientists who study living things

USING *GO* + VERB + *-ING* FOR ACTIVITIES

You can use *go* + verb + *-ing* to describe activities that people do for pleasure. Use this structure in the present, past, and future tenses. Also, use it with modals (such as *can, should,* or *might*) and verbs such as *like, love,* or *hate.*

Examples

> We **went hiking** last weekend.
> You can **go swimming** in Puerto Vallarta.
> I like to **go shopping** if I have money.

Here are some common verbs that use this structure:

bowl	dance	hike	sightsee	surf	window-shop
camp	fish	shop	ski	swim	

11 **Discussing Activities** First, look over the verbs in the list above. Discuss their meanings. For any that you do not know, use a dictionary. Then talk about the activities. Answer the questions below.

1. Which of the activities do you like to do? Why?

2. Which activities do you not like to do? Why?

3. When you travel, do you go sightseeing?

4. Did you do any of these activities last week? Last month? Last year?

5. Are you going to do any of these activities next week? Next month? Next year?

Part 2 Reading Skills and Strategies

Your Travel Personality

Before You Read

1 **Thinking About the Topic** Look at these three photos about different kinds of vacations. Which of the three vacations would *you* like? Write your answer on a piece of paper. Don't tell or show anyone your answer.

A

B

C

2 Previewing Vocabulary Look at the words in the list. They are words from the next reading. Listen to their pronunciation. Do not look them up in a dictionary. Check (✓) the words that you know.

Nouns
- ❑ campfire
- ❑ museum
- ❑ personality
- ❑ relaxing

- ❑ seafood
- ❑ water sports
- ❑ worries (worry)

Adjective
- ❑ boring

Read

3 Completing a Personality Questionnaire Read and answer the following questions.

Your Travel Personality

1. What do you like to do in the morning?
- Ⓐ sleep late
- Ⓑ exercise
- Ⓒ watch TV

2. What do you like to do on Saturday and Sunday?
- Ⓐ go hiking
- Ⓑ go swimming
- Ⓒ go shopping

3. What's most interesting to study when you're on vacation?
- Ⓐ nothing
- Ⓑ animals
- Ⓒ paintings in a museum

4. What do you *not* enjoy?
- Ⓐ a busy, crowded city
- Ⓑ being cold
- Ⓒ sleeping outside

5. It's boring to _____ .
- Ⓐ spend the day at the ocean
- Ⓑ go shopping all day
- Ⓒ do nothing

6. What gives you a headache?
   - Ⓐ hot weather
   - Ⓑ smoke from buses
   - Ⓒ cold air

7. What's most important?
   - Ⓐ clean water
   - Ⓑ clean air
   - Ⓒ a clean bathroom

8. The best food is _____.
   - Ⓐ cooked over a campfire
   - Ⓑ fresh seafood
   - Ⓒ in a good restaurant

9. I like a vacation to be _____.
   - Ⓐ quiet, with no worries
   - Ⓑ exciting, with adventure
   - Ⓒ exciting, with lots of people

10. Which activity do you like best?
   - Ⓐ relaxing
   - Ⓑ water sports
   - Ⓒ sightseeing

After You Read

Strategy

Reaching a Conclusion: Paying Attention to Evidence

Sometimes a reading gives information but doesn't reach a conclusion—a decision or judgment. As the reader, you need to reach this conclusion *yourself*. Pay attention to the evidence (proof) and make an inference. To do this, "add up" all the details in the reading. Come to a conclusion from these details.

4 **Paying Attention to Evidence** Now exchange books with a partner and read each other's answers to the personality questionnaire. What can you guess about your partner's personality? What picture on page 158 do you think your partner would like? Tell your partner. Does your partner agree with your choice? Next, give your partner suggestions.

Examples "You like cities. Maybe you should go to Hong Kong. It's exciting."
"Lake Louise is beautiful. You'll like it."

 5 **Extending the Lesson: Planning Your Dream Vacation** Form a group with 3–4 people who chose the same vacation photo on page 158. Follow these steps:

1. As a group, make a list of all the places in the world that you would like to visit *on your type* of vacation.

2. Each person does *one* of the following:
   - Go to a travel agency and bring back information on *one* of these places.
   - Find a good website with information on *one* of these places.

3. Tell your group what you have learned.

4. As a group, choose one of these places. Plan one perfect day on your "Dream Vacation." Fill in the chart below with that information.

5. Make a report to the class.

Place	Where will you go?	What will you do?	What will you eat?	What will you buy?
Morning				
Afternoon				
Evening				

6 **Writing in Your Journal** Choose one topic below. Write about it for five minutes. Use vocabulary that you learned in this chapter.

- one type of Earthwatch adventure
- your favorite activity
- your idea of the perfect vacation

Tours and Traveling

1 Reading a Website and Discussing Tours Look at the photos on the website below and read about the different tours. Then answer the questions that follow.

A. Whale Watching in Mexico

The Baja Peninsula of Mexico is one of the best places in the world to see whales. Our experienced sea kayakers and biologists will guide you and teach you about whale behavior. You don't need kayaking experience, but you should be in good health. 5
Looking into the eye of a whale is an experience you will not forget.

> Length of trip: 12 days
> Group size: 12
> Cost: $1,100 10

B. Maui Bicycling Tour

Ride a bicycle around one of the most beautiful tropical islands in the world. Swim in the clear, warm tropical water. Camp in the beautiful national parks. Participants provide and carry camping gear, personal gear, and clothing. We provide the bicycles, 15
food, guides and occasional transportation.

> Length of trip: 8 days
> Group size: 8
> Cost: $560

▲ Kayaking in Baja

▲ Bicycling around Maui

▲ Cooking in France

▲ Hiking in the jungle

C. French Cooking Tour

c   Do you like French food? Do you like to cook? Visit   20
Paris and seven other French cities. Eat at some of the best
restaurants in France. Study cooking with some of the most
interesting chefs of France. The price includes food and
hotel as well as one full week of cooking lessons.

    Length of trip: 8 days   25
    Group size: 10
    Cost: $4,560

D. Thailand Jungle Safari

D   This hiking and camping trip provides an adventurous
view of the forests and wildlife of western Thailand. We
make your trip comfortable with our permanent camps.   30
Spend the days exploring the beautiful forests and exciting
animals of Thailand. Spend the nights in our large
comfortable sleeping tents. Take a hot shower and eat
freshly prepared Thai food after a day of hiking.

    Length of trip: 4 days   35
    Group size: 14
    Cost: $650

2 Answering Comprehension Questions Answer the questions about the reading. Discuss your answers with your classmates.

1. Which tour is the most expensive? _____

2. Which tour is the longest? _____

3. Which tour has the most people? _____

4. Which tour is the most interesting to you? _____

5. Which tour is the least interesting to you? _____

3 Making Connections Now read what different people say about their traveling. Then decide which tour is best for each person. Write the letter of the tour in the blank.

1. _____ "I love all kinds of food, but I especially love French food. I want to learn to cook it."

2. _____ "I love adventures! I like to swim, and I want to learn about the ocean."

3. _____ "I like adventure. I have only four days for my vacation."

4. _____ "I'd like to learn something new, and I like Europe."

5. _____ "I like nature and I like to hike, but I really want to be comfortable at night."

6. _____ "I like to swim and ride my bike. I love to go camping."

Part 4 | Vocabulary Practice

1 **Checking Vocabulary** Read these sentences. Check (✓) True or False. New words from this chapter are underlined.

	True	False
1. An <u>adventure</u> is not usually exciting.	❑	❑
2. <u>Biologists</u> study everything from animals to plants.	❑	❑
3. <u>Pollution</u> is often caused by <u>glaciers</u>.	❑	❑
4. <u>Dolphins</u> are mammals that live in the sea.	❑	❑
5. <u>Worried</u> and <u>bored</u> are feelings that people usually don't like to have.	❑	❑
6. <u>Archaeologists</u> are often interested in bones.	❑	❑
7. <u>Tropical climates</u> are not usually warm.	❑	❑
8. Climbing trees is an example of animal <u>behavior</u>.	❑	❑
9. When most people <u>go camping</u>, they stay indoors.	❑	❑
10. People who live on an island probably like <u>seafood</u>.	❑	❑

2 **Listening: Fill in the Missing Words** Listen and fill in the missing words below. Then check your answers on page 154, paragraph D.

Do you enjoy _____ animals? You can spend two
                        1

_____ in Florida. There, you can study dolphins. It will
        2

be _____ to learn about these intelligent ocean _____.
      3   4

These beautiful animals can live to _____ 50 years of age. They
                                          5

travel together in family _____. From small boats, volunteers
                                6

will study and _____ these groups. The purpose of this
                        7

_____ is to learn about the animals' social behavior.
8

Scientists want to know what dolphins do and how they live. Also,

_____ want to study dolphins' health. For example,
9

they wonder, "Is ocean _____ changing the dolphins' health?"
10

If you like warm _____, the ocean, and animals, this is a
11

good _____ for you.
12

3 **Focusing on High-Frequency Words** Read the paragraph below and fill in each blank with a word from the box. Then check your answers in paragraph F on pages 154–155.

adventure	coast	disappearing	plants
amounts	count	enjoy	travel

Do you _____ the beach and like to learn about plants?
1

There is an Earthwatch _____ in Yucatan, Mexico. On the
2

north _____ of Yucatan, there are beautiful species of
3

_____. Unfortunately, many of them are _____.
4 5

People dig them up and sell them for large _____ of money.
6

Mexican biologists need volunteers to collect seeds, _____
7

plants, and help to save several plant species. In your free time, you can

_____ to archaeological sites in the area. If you love a tropical
8

climate, this is the trip for you.

4 **Building Vocabulary** Complete the crossword puzzle. This puzzle uses words from Chapters 8 and 9.

adventure	climate	pollution	species
amount	intelligent	prefer	spend
attractive	irony	raw	together
behavior	obesity	slim	tropical
bored	overweight	southwest	

Across

1. examples: smoke in the air, garbage in the water (n.)
6. a group of living things (n.)
8. how much there is of something (n.)
9. opposite of *ugly* (adj.)
13. the opposite of what we expected (n.)
14. opposite of *fat* (adj.)
16. to like something more than something else (verb)
18. weighing more than average or normal (adj.)
19. a trip that isn't boring at all (n.)

Down

2. condition of very heavy people (n.)
3. We do this with time and money. (v.)
4. the way we act (n.)
5. You're in eastern Canada. Which direction is Mexico? (adj.)
7. smart, like dolphins, for example (adj.)
10. examples: temperature, rain, wind (n.)
11. opposite of *apart* (adj.)
12. Palm trees, warm weather, and rain forests are in _____ climates. (adj.)
15. not cooked (adj)
17. not interested (adj.)

KEY: *adj.* = adjective; *adv.* = adverb; *n.* = noun; *prep.* = preposition; *v.* = verb

Self-Assessment Log

Read the lists below. Check (✓) the strategies and vocabulary that you know. Look through the chapter or ask your instructor about the other strategies and words.

Reading and Vocabulary-Building Strategies

- ❏ Understanding words for direction
- ❏ Finding the main idea
- ❏ Finding details
- ❏ Understanding words from their prefixes
- ❏ Using *go* + verb + *-ing* for activities
- ❏ Reaching a conclusion: paying attention to evidence
- ❏ Reading a website

Target Vocabulary

Nouns

- ❏ adventure*
- ❏ amount*
- ❏ archaeologists
- ❏ behavior
- ❏ biologists
- ❏ campfire
- ❏ climate
- ❏ coast*
- ❏ dolphins
- ❏ glaciers
- ❏ museum
- ❏ ocean
- ❏ personality
- ❏ plants*
- ❏ pollution
- ❏ prehistory
- ❏ relaxing
- ❏ seafood
- ❏ species
- ❏ water sports
- ❏ worries (worry)
- ❏ weather

Verbs

- ❏ count*
- ❏ disappearing*
- ❏ go camping
- ❏ go sightseeing
- ❏ prefer
- ❏ travel*

Adjectives

- ❏ bored
- ❏ boring
- ❏ intelligent
- ❏ tropical
- ❏ worried

Adverb

- ❏ together*

* These words are among the 1,000 most-frequently used words in English.

10

Our Planet

We all live here. Where is it? Planet Earth! In this chapter, you will read about the environment. In Part 1, you will read about environmental problems in the ocean and will have a chance to discuss solutions and opinions. In Part 2, you will learn about things that we can do to help save the environment. As you know, people in all countries produce garbage, but some countries produce more than others. Which countries produce the most garbage? What do people throw out? What do they recycle? Part 3 helps answer these questions. Part 4 gives you a chance to further work with new vocabulary.

❝ The survival of the world depends upon our sharing what we have and working together. If we don't, the whole world will die. First the planet, and next the people. ❞

—Frank Fools Crow
Ceremonial Chief of the Native American nation, Teton Sioux (1890–1989)

Connecting to the Topic

1 What do you see in this photo? What do you think the men are doing?

2 Why is it important to plant trees?

3 Name five things that you think are harmful to the planet. Name five things you think are helpful.

The Ocean in Trouble

Before You Read

1 Thinking About the Topic Look at the photos and answer the questions.

▲ Seafood for restaurants

▲ Fishers repairing their nets

▲ Commercial fishing trawler with its nets

1. Describe each photo. What do you see?

2. Which countries have a lot of coastline, lakes, and rivers? Do you think fishing is important in those places?

3. Do you eat a lot of seafood? Do you think people eat more seafood now than they ate in the past? If so, why?

4. Do you know of any problems for the fishing industry?

2 Previewing Vocabulary Read the words in the list. They are words from the next reading. Listen to their pronunciation. Do not look them up in a dictionary. Check (✓) the words that you know.

Nouns	Verbs	Adjectives	Preposition
❑ amount	❑ catch	❑ extinct	❑ but
❑ areas	❑ create	❑ fake	
❑ crabs	❑ destroy		
❑ damage	❑ drag		
❑ danger	❑ influence		
❑ dolphins	❑ police		
❑ environmentalists	❑ pressure		
❑ methods	❑ prove		
❑ nets	❑ reproduce		
❑ overfishing	❑ urged		
❑ trawlers	❑ warning		
❑ whales			
❑ zones			

3 Finding the Meaning of Words from Context Find the meanings of the underlined words. Look at the sentence or phrase before or after the word for help.

1. George loves to eat, and he likes all kinds of food. He'll eat anything but insects because he thinks they're disgusting.
   - (A) however
   - (B) except for
   - (C) and

2. The large boat dragged another small boat behind it through the water.
   - (A) pulled
   - (B) pushed
   - (C) repaired

3. Our great-grandparents sometimes saw that species, but now we can't because it's extinct, like the dinosaurs.
   - (A) hard to find
   - (B) completely dead
   - (C) only in zoos

4. After the people of the city pressured the government, the government built a new road.
   - (A) caused worry to
   - (B) caused stress to
   - (C) put a lot of stress on

5. At first, the biologists made suggestions. The government didn't do anything about the problem, however, so now the biologists are <u>urging</u> the government to do something.

    Ⓐ doing more research

    Ⓑ hoping

    Ⓒ strongly asking

6. "If you eat that, you'll get sick," he <u>warned</u> me.

    Ⓐ predicted something bad

    Ⓑ asked

    Ⓒ showed

Read

4 **Reading an Article** Read the following article. Don't use your dictionary. If you don't know some words, try to figure out their meanings. Then do the exercises.

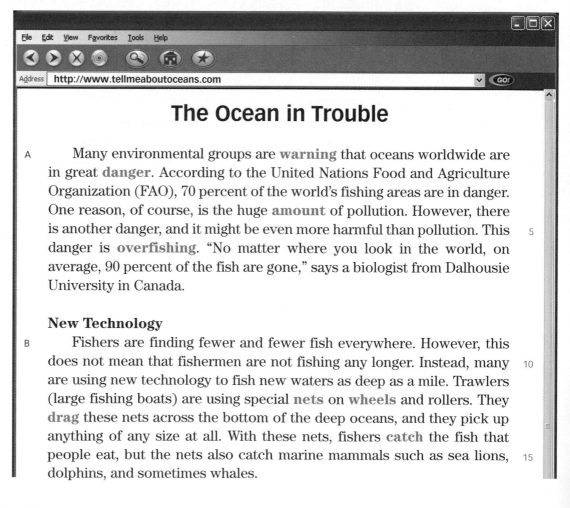

The Ocean in Trouble

A   Many environmental groups are **warning** that oceans worldwide are in great **danger**. According to the United Nations Food and Agriculture Organization (FAO), 70 percent of the world's fishing areas are in danger. One reason, of course, is the huge **amount** of pollution. However, there is another danger, and it might be even more harmful than pollution. This   5 danger is **overfishing**. "No matter where you look in the world, on average, 90 percent of the fish are gone," says a biologist from Dalhousie University in Canada.

New Technology

B   Fishers are finding fewer and fewer fish everywhere. However, this does not mean that fishermen are not fishing any longer. Instead, many   10 are using new technology to fish new waters as deep as a mile. Trawlers (large fishing boats) are using special **nets** on **wheels** and rollers. They **drag** these nets across the bottom of the deep oceans, and they pick up anything of any size at all. With these nets, fishers **catch** the fish that people eat, but the nets also catch marine mammals such as sea lions,   15 dolphins, and sometimes whales.

The Effect on Fish

C   These nets also take species like squid, skate, red **crabs**, slackjaw eels, spiny dogfish, and orange roughy. A few years ago, people didn't want to eat these species. Now you can find them in fish stores, in fish sandwiches at fast-food restaurants, or in **fake**—not real— "crab meat" for seafood salads. The orange roughy provides an example of what is happening. This fish appeared in fish stores **only** about ten years ago, but already the species is almost **extinct**. The orange roughy lives very deep in the ocean—up to a mile deep—in the cold waters off New Zealand.

▲ Crab is more expensive than other seafood, so the "crab" in your crab salad might be fake.

Scientists now know that fish in deep cold water grow and **reproduce** very slowly. For example, the orange roughy lives to be 150 years old. It doesn't start to reproduce until it is 30 years old. Although the fish is nearly extinct, people still sell it in seafood stores and in restaurants. And, of course, it may be in that fish sandwich that you eat at a fast-food restaurant.

D   Many scientists believe that present fishing **methods** will **destroy** all the large fishing areas of the world. Can anything stop this? Some scientists think that governments should stop the fishing industry from using some kinds of technology. But this will be difficult. Many of the big fishing companies have a lot of money, and they use that money to **influence** politicians all around the world.

No Fishing Zones

E   Other scientists believe that governments should **create** no-fishing zones—areas where no one can fish. Governments can **police** these areas. During the U.N. International Year of the Ocean, more than 1,600 leading marine scientists and conservation biologists from 65 countries **urged** the world to create 80 times the no-fishing areas that exist now. Their goal is to protect 20 percent of the world's oceans by the year 2020. This is happening in some places; for example, the fishing industry in Britain is beginning to accept no-fishing zones because the amount of fish that the industry catches is getting smaller and smaller.

F   The fishing industry often argues that the scientific evidence is not complete—that we just don't know what is going on in the oceans. Now, scientists and **environmentalists** have to give evidence to show that the fishing industry is doing **damage** before the government will pass laws protecting the ocean. This takes time, and sometimes it is difficult to **prove** something like this. The magazine *Science* says we should have the opposite rule: big fishing companies should have to prove that they are *not* destroying the oceans before we allow them to fish.

Conclusion

G   Environmentalists say that average people need to get together and **pressure** their governments to do something. The large fishing companies that own the big trawlers are not going to stop fishing by themselves. The environmentalists say that if we don't pressure our governments, there will be nothing left in the oceans **but** water.   60

After You Read

5 **Making Inferences** Make an inference about the writer's purpose in "The Ocean in Trouble." Why did he write this? Choose the answer below.

- (A) to give the reader information about why the fishing industry is important
- (B) to help the reader understand how the fishing industry works and also understand about deep water fish like the orange roughy
- (C) to tell the reader about the problems caused by overfishing and suggest possible solutions
- (D) to tell the reader about the problems of ocean pollution

6 **Finding the Main Idea** The main idea of the reading is that _____

_____

_____ .

7 **Working with New Words** Write the vocabulary words for the meanings below. For help, look back at the boldfaced words in the reading.

Paragraph	Meaning	Word
C	have babies	
E	areas	
F	people who work to take care of the environment	
F	give evidence to show that something is true	

Strategy

Understanding Words from Their Parts: *Over* in a Word
Some parts of words can help you to understand the meaning of the word. *Over* is such a word. At the beginning of a word, *over* can mean "too much" or "more than is good."

Example
    One great danger to oceans worldwide is **overfishing**.

        (You see that *overfishing* means "taking too many fish from the ocean.")

8 **Understanding Words from Their Parts** Can you figure out a word for each blank below? Use *over* in each word. Follow the example.

1. If you did too much and got tired, you ___*overdid*___ it.

2. If you eat too much, you might get sick because it's not good to _____.

3. It's not a good idea to work too much. Please try not to _____.

4. If you sleep too late, you will be late for work. Set your alarm clock so you don't
_____.

5. If you spend too much money on clothes, you might not have enough for food.
It's a good idea to have a budget so that you don't _____.

UNDERSTANDING WORDS THAT CAN BE MORE THAN ONE PART OF SPEECH

Many words in English can be more than one part of speech. For example, a word might be both a noun and a verb. Often, the meaning is similar. Sometimes it's different.

Examples

There aren't enough **police** in this city.
> (In this sentence, *police* is a noun. It means *people whose job is protecting the public*.)

Governments have to **police** the oceans.
> (Here, *police* is a verb. It means *to keep order in a place*.)

9 **Understanding Words That Can Be More Than One Part of Speech**
What is the part of speech of each underlined word—noun or verb?

                                                                        Part of Speech

1. They shouldn't <u>fish</u> in that area.   _____

2. I eat <u>fish</u> several times a week.   _____

3. In the future, there might be nothing in the ocean
   but <u>water</u>.   _____

4. In hot weather, you need to <u>water</u> the garden every day.   _____

5. They don't usually <u>catch</u> many fish any more.   _____

6. Their <u>catch</u> of fish was good this week.   _____

7. There is a lot of <u>pressure</u> on the fishing industry.   _____

8. Environmental groups often <u>pressure</u> the fishing industry
   to do things differently.   _____

Understanding Relationships Between Ideas

Understanding the relationship between ideas and details in a reading is important. You can use graphic organizers or charts to help. Some are simple. Others are more complicated. They can help you to "see" ideas. If you put information from a reading on a graphic organizer, it can help you to study for exams. You will practice using a graphic organizer below.

10 **Understanding Relationships Between Ideas** Below is a graphic organizer about "The Ocean in Trouble." Look back at the reading on pages 172–174 and fill in the missing information.

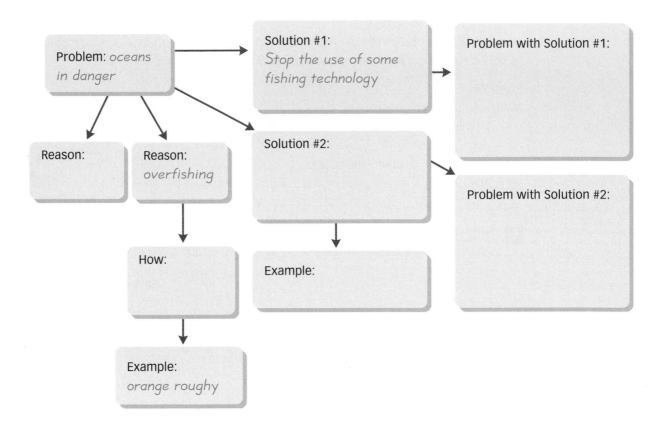

11 **Discussing the Reading** Talk about your answers to the following questions.

1. What solution to the problem of overfishing does the writer give at the end of the article? In your opinion, is this a good idea? Why or why not?

2. The writer writes about two groups—the fishing industry and environmentalists. Which group does the writer agree with? Why do you think this? (Find evidence for your answer in the reading.)

Repairing the Environment

1 **Interviewing** Read the two questions in the chart below. Write your own question about the environment. Decide on your answers. Then walk around the room and ask three students these questions. Write their answers in the chart.

Questions	Student 1	Student 2	Student 3
1. What are problems with the environment in your city, state, province, or country?			
2. What prediction can you make about the environment 50 years in the future?			
3. *(Your question)*			

2 **Previewing Vocabulary** Read the words in the list. They are words from the next reading. Listen to their pronunciation. Do not look them up in a dictionary. Check (✓) the words that you know.

Nouns
- ❏ canoes
- ❏ cloth bag
- ❏ containers
- ❏ damage
- ❏ garbage
- ❏ island
- ❏ plastic bags

- ❏ statues
- ❏ stone
- ❏ trash
- ❏ vegetation

Verbs
- ❏ absorb
- ❏ arrived

- ❏ build
- ❏ cut down
- ❏ last
- ❏ melting
- ❏ mention
- ❏ produce
- ❏ recycle
- ❏ stopped

Adjectives
- ❏ amazing
- ❏ ancient
- ❏ organic
- ❏ plastic
- ❏ surrounding

3 Reading an Article Read this article.

Repairing the Environment

Early Life on Easter Island

A   Easter Island is a very small **island** in the Pacific Ocean. In the **ancient** past, the island was covered with **vegetation**, such as beautiful forests, and the **surrounding** ocean was rich in fish. The human population grew to about 9,000 people. Today, we know them for their art—hundreds of huge, **amazing statues** that are made of **stone**. Over several hundred years, the people created larger and larger statues. 5

The Changing History

▲ At one time, Easter Island was covered with vegetation and forests. The people created amazing stone statues.

B   For about 700 years, life on Easter Island was good. However, by the 15th century, people suddenly **stopped** creating the statues. Also, the environment completely changed. The earth didn't **produce** enough food for the 10 population. The forests were gone because people **cut down** all the trees. Without trees, they couldn't even **build canoes**—a kind of small boat—and for this reason, they couldn't go fishing. The society was destroyed. The people were hungry. When Europeans 15 **arrived** in 1722, there were only about 2,000 people left.

Easter Island as an Example

C   Scientists often **mention** Easter Island. They see it as an example of the **damage** that humans can do to the environment. They say that our Earth is like an island. When we destroy it, we destroy ourselves. They say that we are now destroying it. Like the people of ancient Easter Island, we 20 are cutting down forests. Worldwide, the environment is changing. The climate is becoming warmer. Glaciers are **melting**. Pollution fills many rivers and lakes and the air of many cities. And every year, about 20,000 plant and animal species become extinct.

What We Can Do

D   Some people see this situation as hopeless, but environmentalists say 25 that it isn't too late. There *are* things that we can do. Governments and big companies need to make big changes, but every individual can make many small changes. All these small changes can add up. They can make a big difference. Here are just some:

▲ Paper, plastic, or cloth?

- Plant trees. Trees **absorb** ("drink in") the carbon dioxide (CO_2) that factories put into the air. 30

- Buy **organic** fruits and vegetables—ones without dangerous chemicals. These are good for your health and good for the earth, too.

- Reuse **containers**; in other words, don't throw 35 empty **plastic** food containers into the **trash** or **garbage**. Wash them and use them again. Also, use **plastic bags** many times. When you throw away a plastic bag or container, it stays in the earth for *thousands of years*.

- Don't use paper *or* plastic bags. Bring a **cloth bag** with you to the 40 supermarket. You can use the same cloth bag over and over for years.

- **Recycle** things that you can't reuse. You can recycle aluminum cans, glass bottles, some plastic containers, and newspapers.

- Use compact fluorescent light bulbs. They **last** ten times longer than regular light bulbs, so they save you money. Also, they use 75 percent 45 less energy. One of these bulbs can keep 1/2 ton (1,000 pounds) of carbon dioxide out of the air.

▲ A compact fluorescent light bulb

▲ A regular light bulb

▲ Is your tuna fish dolphin-safe?

- Do you eat tuna fish? If so, look carefully at the can. Buy only tuna that is dolphin-safe—in other words, tuna from companies with special nets that don't 50 kill dolphins.

- Write letters to government leaders. Ask them for laws that protect the environment. Tell them that you want the earth to be here for your great-great grandchildren. 55

4 Finding the Main Idea Read the sentences below. Which one is the main idea of "Repairing the Environment"?

- (A) In the past, Easter Island had a beautiful environment, but the people destroyed it when they cut down all the trees.
- (B) There are things that individual people can do to help the environment.
- (C) Some environmentalists think that the situation is hopeless, but others say that it's not too late to save the earth.
- (D) If we make some changes in the way that we live, we don't have to repeat the mistake of the people of Easter Island, who destroyed their environment.

5 Working with New Words Write the vocabulary words for the meanings below. For help, look back at the boldfaced words in the reading.

Paragraph	Meaning	Word
A	a type of art	
B	a type of small boat	
C	changing from ice to water	
D	drink in	
D	use something again; reuse	

6 Finding Details Look back at Paragraphs B and C for the answers to these questions.

1. Why couldn't the people of Easter Island go fishing?

2. Why couldn't they build canoes?

3. What is happening to the earth's environment today?

7 Discussing the Reading Talk about your answers to the following questions.

1. Look at the list in Paragraph D of the reading. Do you do any of those things? If so, which ones? Are there other things that you do?

2. What's good about organic fruits and vegetables? Can you think of a possible problem with them?

3. Does your city have a recycling program? If so, talk about it with your group.

8 **Writing in Your Journal** Choose one topic below. Write about it for five minutes. Use vocabulary that you learned in this chapter.

- something that you learned about the ocean
- something that you learned about Easter Island
- your ideas on ways to help the environment

Part 3 | Practical English

Using Facts and Figures

1 **Reading a Graph** The graph below tells how many pounds of garbage a person makes on each day in eleven cities. Look at the graph and answer the questions.

Pounds of Garbage Produced per Person per Day

Los Angeles	6.4
Philadelphia	5.8
Chicago	5.0
New York	4.0
Tokyo	3.0
Paris	2.4
Toronto	2.4
Hamburg	1.9
Rome	1.5
Calcutta	1.12
Kano, Nigeria	1.0

1. Who makes more garbage each day—a person in Tokyo or New York City?

   _____

2. Who makes more garbage each day—a person in Toronto or Los Angeles?

   _____

3. Who makes more garbage each day—a person in Calcutta or Paris?

   _____

2 Comparing Facts and Figures in a Graph Choose the best answer to complete the sentences.

1. Five people in Kano, Nigeria, make the same amount of garbage each day as

   _____.

   Ⓐ two people in Rome
   Ⓑ one person in Chicago
   Ⓒ two people in Toronto

2. Five people in Calcutta, India, make about the same amount of garbage as

   _____.

   Ⓐ three people in Los Angeles
   Ⓑ two people in Chicago
   Ⓒ one person in Philadelphia

FYI

Note: 16 oz. = 1
pound = 2.2 kilos

3 Reading a Paragraph with a Chart Read about Kenji and Tanya. Then answer the questions. Refer to the graph on page 181.

Kenji recycles his metal cans. He takes them to a recycling center so they can be used again. He doesn't throw any in the garbage. He recycles his paper products. He puts his yard waste in a pile and puts it on his garden later. Here is a list of what he put in the garbage today.

metal cans	0 oz.
food waste	8 oz.
yard waste	0 oz.
paper products	0 oz.
glass bottles, jars, etc.	16 oz.

1. How much garbage did Kenji throw away? _____

2. That is the average for what city? _____

Tanya likes to read the newspaper and work in the yard. Sometimes she recycles and sometimes she doesn't. Tanya throws out a lot of things. Today she threw out the following things.

bottles	14 oz.
soda cans and tin cans	8 oz.
one newspaper, some letters, a magazine	30 oz.
extra food	12 oz.
yard waste	16 oz.

1. How many pounds of garbage did Tanya throw out? (Hint: Add the total ounces, then divide by 16.)

_____

2. Tanya's garbage was exactly average for her city. Where does Tanya live?

_____

How about you? What did you throw out or recycle yesterday? Make a list.

_____   _____

_____   _____

_____   _____

_____   _____

_____   _____

4 **Reading a Pie Chart** Garbage is created all over the world every day. Look at this pie chart about garbage in the U.S. Answer the questions on page 184.

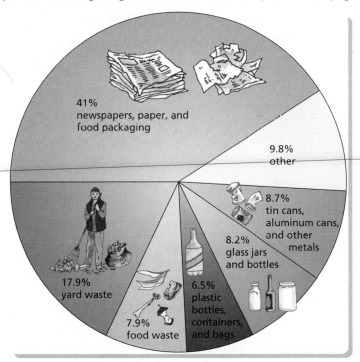

▲ Breakdown of garbage in the U.S.

1. In the U.S. is there a larger percentage of newspapers or plastic bottles?

There is a larger percentage of newspapers.

2. What percentage is larger: yard waste or tin cans?

_____

3. What percentage is greater: glass or plastic bottles?

_____

4. What percentage of the trash are metal cans and other metals?

_____

5. What percentage of the trash are grass clippings and other yard waste?

_____

6. What percentage of the trash is food waste?

_____

Part 4   Vocabulary Practice

1 Building Vocabulary Match the words and phrases that go together.

1. _h_ dolphins   a. about danger

2. _____ catch   b. zones

3. _____ extinct   c. have babies

4. _____ amount   d. gone from the earth

5. _____ ancient   e. very old

6. _____ areas   f. with a net

7. _____ pressure   g. influence

8. _____ warning   h. mammals

9. _____ wheels   i. rollers

10. _____ reproduce   j. percentage

2 Using Words in Sentences Write new sentences using the words next to each number. You can look at the readings in Parts 1 and 2 if you need help.

1. warn / scientists / oceans

Scientists warned us that the oceans are in trouble.

2. extinct / species

_____

3. money / influence / government

_____

4. methods / destroy / fishing areas

_____

5. pollution / overfishing / oceans

_____

6. environmentalists / damage / prove

_____

7. Easter Island / trees

_____

8. reproduce / cold water / slowly

_____

9. canoes / fishing

_____

3 **Listening: Focusing on High-Frequency Words** Listen and fill in the blanks in the sentences. Then check your answers on page 178, paragraph B.

> For about 700 years, life on Easter Island was good. However, by the 15th century, people suddenly _____ creating the statues. Also, the environment completely changed. The earth didn't _____ enough food for the _____. The forests were gone because people _____ all the trees. Without trees, they couldn't even _____ canoes—a kind of small boat—and for this reason, they couldn't go _____. The society was destroyed. The people were hungry. When Europeans _____ in 1722, there were _____ about 2,000 people left.

4 **Building Vocabulary** Complete the crossword puzzle. This puzzle uses words from Chapters 9 and 10.

ancient	climate	influence	ocean	pressure	seed	urge
behavior	extinct	island	overfish	prove	statue	warn
bored	fake	nets	pollution	reproduce	stone	zone

5 Building Vocabulary Complete the crossword puzzle. This puzzle uses words from Chapters 9 and 10.

Across

2. example: weather that is cold in winter, warm in summer (n.)
4. examples: eating, communicating, fighting, reproducing (n.)
6. junk that people put in the air, sea, etc. (n.)
8. Lawyers have to _____ that a criminal is guilty. (v.)
11. Ancient people used tools made of this. (n.)
12. very old, in the far past (adj.)
14. things used to catch butterflies or fish (n.)
16. ask someone strongly (v.)
17. have babies (v.)
18. area made for a special purpose (n.)

19. not alive anywhere on the earth anymore (adj.)

Down

1. A plant begins from this. (n.)
3. land surrounded by water (n.)
5. use power over someone or something (v.)
7. not real (adj.)
8. put a lot of stress on someone to do something (v.)
9. example: Pacific, Atlantic (n.)
10. opposite of excited (adj.)
11. example: a huge sculpture, found on Easter Island (n.)
13. catch too many fish (v.)
15. tell someone about danger (v.)

KEY: *adj.* = adjective; *adv.* = adverb; *n.* = noun; *prep.* = preposition; *v.* = verb

Self-Assessment Log

Read the lists below. Check (✓) the strategies and vocabulary that you know. Look through the chapter or ask your instructor about the other strategies and words.

Reading and Vocabulary-Building Strategies

- ❑ Finding the meaning of words from context
- ❑ Making inferences
- ❑ Finding the main idea
- ❑ Understanding words from their parts: *over* in a word
- ❑ Understanding words that can be more than one part of speech
- ❑ Understanding relationships between ideas
- ❑ Finding details
- ❑ Reading a graph
- ❑ Comparing facts and figures in a graph
- ❑ Reading a paragraph with a chart
- ❑ Reading a pie chart

Target Vocabulary

Nouns

- ❑ amount*
- ❑ areas
- ❑ canoes
- ❑ damage
- ❑ danger*
- ❑ environmentalists
- ❑ island
- ❑ nets
- ❑ overfishing
- ❑ statues
- ❑ stone*
- ❑ zones

Verbs

- ❑ absorb
- ❑ arrived*
- ❑ build*
- ❑ catch*
- ❑ cut down*
- ❑ destroy*
- ❑ drag
- ❑ influence*
- ❑ police*
- ❑ pressure*
- ❑ produce*
- ❑ prove*
- ❑ recycle
- ❑ reproduce
- ❑ stopped*
- ❑ urged
- ❑ warning

Adjectives

- ❑ extinct
- ❑ fake

Adverb

- ❑ only*

Preposition

- ❑ but*

*These words are among the 1,000 most-frequently used words in English.

Vocabulary Index

---

*These words are among the 1,000 most frequently used words in English

conversations
equal*
feelings*
full-time
hierarchy
lonely
orders*
politics*
position*
private*
public*
sexism
similar
socialize
spouse
suggestions*
uninteresting

Chapter 6

anxious
awake
childhood*
complicated
desires*
emotions
evidence
familiar*
Freud
hormone
however
logic
make sense
occurs
outside*
predict
psychologists
purpose*
realized*
repair
research
stage*
symbols
theories
    (theory)
traveling*
unfamiliar
vision
wonder*

Chapter 7

AIDS
contrast
crime
daily*
delivering
drugs
email
energy
environment
famous*
fun
hardships*
homeless*
homelessness
lives (life) *
lonely
mammals
planted*
prepare*
release
street children
take care of
taught (teach) *
teenagers
tough
volunteer
world

Chapter 8

attractive
bake
boil
bugs
calories (calorie)
centers*
dairy
delicious
diabetes
disgusting
doctors*
entomologists
except*
fried
fry
gain*
insects
irony

join*
lose*
marinate
obesity
people*
protein
raw*
slim
snacks
spend*
thousands*
ugly
while
worldwide

Chapter 9

adventure*
amount*
archaeologists
behavior
biologists
bored
boring
campfire
climate
coast*
count*
disappearing
    (disappear) *
dolphins
glaciers
go camping
go sightseeing
intelligent
museum
ocean
personality
plants*
pollution
prefer
prehistory
relaxing
seafood
species
together*
travel*
tropical
water sports

weather
worried
worries (worry)

Chapter 10

absorb
amount*
areas
arrived*
build*
but*
canoes
catch*
cut down*
damage
danger*
destroy*
drag
environmentalists
extinct
fake
influence*
island
nets
only*
overfishing
police*
pressure*
produce*
prove*
recycle
reproduce
statues
stone*
stopped*
urged
warning
zones

---

*These words are among the 1,000 most frequently used words in English

Skills Index